THE GATHERING HOME

CREATING A REFUGE
OF GOODNESS AND JOY

EMILY BELLE FREEMAN

With Katie Wilson Hughes and Jessica Kettle, contributors

DESERET BOOK

SALT LAKE CITY, UTAH

TO JEANNE KESLER, VALERIE HAWKINS, BONNIE FREEMAN, AND MY OWN
DEAR MOM, WHO TAUGHT ME THE BEAUTIFUL WAY OF WELCOMING IN.

—*Emily*

TO MY MOM, BECKY, WHO CONTINUALLY SHOWS ME WHAT IT MEANS
TO HAVE A GATHERING HOME AND A GATHERING HEART, AND WHOSE
TABLE ALWAYS HAS ROOM FOR ONE MORE.

—*Jess*

TO MY MOTHER, GAYLE, WHO LIVED AND TAUGHT THE TRUE
ART OF GATHERING.

—*Katie*

All photographs © Jessica Kettle
Book design © Deseret Book Company
Book cover and interior design by Brooke Baird Williams

© 2020 Emily Belle Freeman LC; Jessica Kettle; and Katie Wilson Hughes

All rights reserved. No part of this book may be reproduced in any form or by any means without permission in writing from the publisher, Deseret Book Company, at permissions@deseretbook.com or PO Box 30178, Salt Lake City, Utah 84130. This work is not an official publication of The Church of Jesus Christ of Latter-day Saints. The views expressed herein are the responsibility of the authors and do not necessarily represent the position of the Church or of Deseret Book Company.

Deseret Book is a registered trademark of Deseret Book Company.

Visit us at deseretbook.com

Library of Congress Cataloging-in-Publication Data
(CIP data on file)
ISBN 978-1-62972-822-3

Printed in China
RR Donnelley, Dongguan, China

10 9 8 7 6 5 4 3 2 1

CONTENTS

Introduction

GATHERING IN	3
THE HOSPITALITY CODE	9
AN OFFERING	13
BUILDING THE REFUGE	19

PART ONE
The Sacred in the Everyday

PRAYER	31
SCRIPTURE	35
THE SABBATH	39
MEALTIMES	43
RITES OF PASSAGE	49

PART TWO
The Celebration of Seasons

JANUARY	54
FEBRUARY	60
MARCH	64
APRIL	70
MAY	76
JUNE	80
JULY	84
AUGUST	90
SEPTEMBER	94
OCTOBER	100
NOVEMBER	104
DECEMBER	110

Planning Pages

THE SACRED IN THE EVERYDAY 119
RITES OF PASSAGE 225
THE CELEBRATION OF SEASONS 233
GENERAL CONFERENCE 259

REFERENCES 264

INTRODUCTION

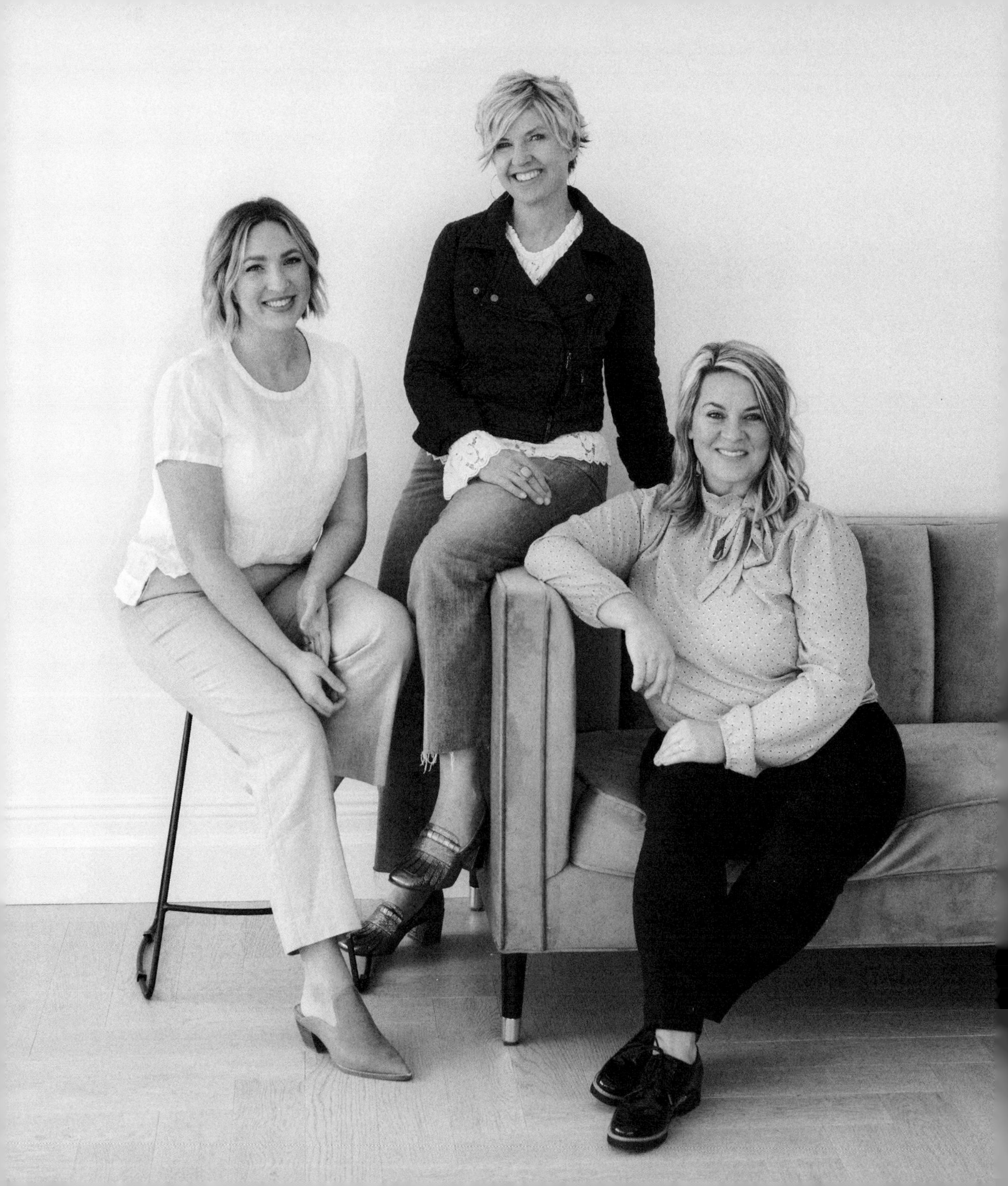

Gathering In

Every so often we are given the invitation to slow down. Time stands still, and we see the smiles and hear the easy conversation and the sound of sweet laughter. These are our people, our moments, our memories.

There is an art of gathering–of welcoming in. Those moments of stillness become sacred when we spend time making people feel special and cared for. "Gathering" is familiar traditions handed down: fresh flowers on the table, homemade cookies on the counter, the candle lit just before scripture study begins. It's the little things, the thoughtfulness and attention to detail, that make memories meaningful.

Gathering doesn't require a holiday. It can be inviting friends over for lunch or a new family over for dessert. Hot chocolate for breakfast on the first day of snow. Spontaneous stargazing on the back lawn at midnight.

Gathering is inviting people into your life, instilling a sense of belonging. It is an expression of love. For us, bringing people together is an art we are passionate about. The art of hospitality. The essence of gathering in.

WHO WE ARE

Emily Belle Freeman

What you need to know first and foremost about me is that I love to gather people. I am not great at details or decorations, but I find an abundance of happiness in loving well. I believe there is a strength that comes when we gather together that can't be found in any other way. It is not the particulars of the celebration that matter to me; it's all about the people. Perhaps the best illustration of this is the year our family celebrated Christmas in March because it was the only weekend the whole family could be together. I put up the tree and the stockings. We played Christmas music and served our favorite holiday foods. We wore Christmas pajamas and celebrated just the way we would have in December. It is one of my favorite memories because everyone was there. My five children will tell you that focusing on people and finding the meaning behind the moment are far more important to me than sticking to a date on a calendar. Gathering is all about bringing in the sacred. It is inviting the Spirit of Christ into the everyday and the seasonal celebrations of our story. My greatest belief about gathering is that it is a tool that enables us to create a Christ-centered home where everyone is welcome.

Create a Christ-centered home where everyone is welcome

Jessica Kettle

Meet my friend Jess. She is a professional photographer, editor, and creator of Jess Kettle Presets. Her work has taken her everywhere, from the Ozarks to Aruba, and she has been featured on Martha Stewart's website and in *Good Housekeeping* and *The Knot* magazines. She has four kids and loves girls' nights out and spending summer days at the lake with her family. As a working mom, Jess often finds herself second-guessing how she spends the hours and minutes of her days. She knows what it feels like to be spread too thin and to set overwhelming expectations for herself. Jess used to be a party perfectionist who would obsess over every detail of a special event or gathering, including the perfect menu, the most unusual party theme, and picture-worthy décor. As it turned out, that perfectionism brought more stress than joy for her and her family. Her gathering style has evolved over time as she has settled into motherhood and accepted the fact that her family cares more about being together than about a picture-perfect event. She goes big for birthdays, Halloween, and Christmas but still sends invitations via text message. She has become the queen of last-minute, quickly planned soirees. You won't find elaborate tablescapes or mantel decorations every month of the year at her house, but you will find Sunday dinners with neighbors, late evenings filled with laughter as everyone squishes together on family-room couches, and people gathered around the kitchen counter in meaningful conversation. Her greatest belief about gathering is that we can choose connection over perfection.

Choose connection over perfection

Katie Wilson Hughes

I can't wait to introduce you to my friend Katie. She is someone I admire because no one creates the magic of gathering in the same way she does. Her love for gathering was passed down through the women in her family, and the art of hospitality was taught to her by her mother. Katie believes that love is in the little things. She loves to send the invite, beautify the space, create the visual, and magnify the moment down to the last detail. She believes that putting energy, time, and thought into a gathering makes people feel thought of, remembered, and known. For her, the greatest expression of love is turning an ordinary space into something extraordinary. She has a gift for decorating beautiful spaces on a limited income, using things found in nature, old ribbons she's been hanging onto, or items from the thrift store. Celebrating is all about creating love in the gathering spaces: the mantel, the buffet, the dining table, the front door. It's creating the magic her loved ones will feel in the first minute of the celebration. Her greatest belief about gathering is that we can create a space that lets people know they are loved.

Create a space that lets people know they are loved

Jess and Katie will share their suggestions for gathering in part 2 of this book. You will love the balance they bring between valuing connection over perfection and remembering the details. The three of us love planning gatherings together, and you can find more of our ideas on Instagram @the.gatheringhome.

HOW TO USE THIS BOOK

This book is filled to bursting with ideas for every sort of gathering—both the holiday traditions and the sacred everyday routines—but they are not meant to overwhelm you. We recognize that sometimes people put undue pressure on themselves when they think of creating a gathering space. They might focus more on what the pictures will look like than on the people who will gather. Instead, we invite you to forget about the camera and work to create something simple but meaningful for the ones you love. We will give you all the ideas we can with an invitation to start small until you find the style that speaks to you. Set aside the need for perfection; replace it with the ideal of making memories. Focus on the feeling in your home, on the welcoming, and let that become more important than elaborate decorations or fancy recipes or a freshly mopped floor. For us, gathering is all about the inviting in. Don't wait for the perfect opportunity; instead, let gathering become your way of life.

The ideas in this book are meant for anyone, in any stage of life. You can use them as a family or as a group of friends, as single adults or as empty nesters. You might use some of these ideas for youth activities or even neighborhood get-togethers. We envision aunts inviting nieces and nephews into their homes, friends gathering friends, and families creating memories. We have included more ideas than you might use in one season with the hope that this book will become an ongoing resource to be used over the years and with many different groups of people.

Part 1, written by Emily, discusses the sacred in the everyday. It focuses on inviting the Spirit of Christ into the daily and weekly gatherings of a home. In this section, we will talk about prayer, scripture, mealtimes, Sabbath days, and rites of passage and introduce you to planning pages that will help you be more intentional and Christ-centered in your daily and weekly gatherings. These planning worksheets for "The Sacred in the Everyday" can be found in the Planning Pages section at the back of the book. You will find enough planning pages for every week of the year.

Part 2 is a compilation of our very favorite holiday-gathering ideas. This section was written by all three of us and is devoted to helping you create deliberate monthly gatherings for your family, friends, or neighbors. Here you will find ideas for seasonal holidays and gatherings that will help you build a refuge of hospitality and celebration. Some of these ideas come from gatherings the three of us have individually experienced in our own homes, either with our present families or as we were growing up. Others are ideas we have collected over the years and would love to try someday. Some of the gathering suggestions are a combination of ideas from each of our own individual traditions.

Although every idea in this book is a compilation, we will put the name of the person who inspired the gathering idea under each post in part 2 so that you know whose idea is whose. Because of where Jess, Katie, and I are from, many of the traditions described in this book fit within American culture. If you live outside of the United States, replace some of our traditional holiday celebrations with some of yours! Our hope is that these ideas will be a starting place for you to consider and build upon as you create gatherings that are perfect for the people you love.

Just like part 1, part 2 is supplemented by a set of planning pages, including worksheets for holidays and general conference. You can find these monthly planning pages in the Planning Pages section at the end of the book under "The Celebration of Seasons" and "General Conference."

We hope this will be a year of gathering in, of extending the welcome, of instilling a sense of belonging.

Are you ready?

Let the gathering begin.

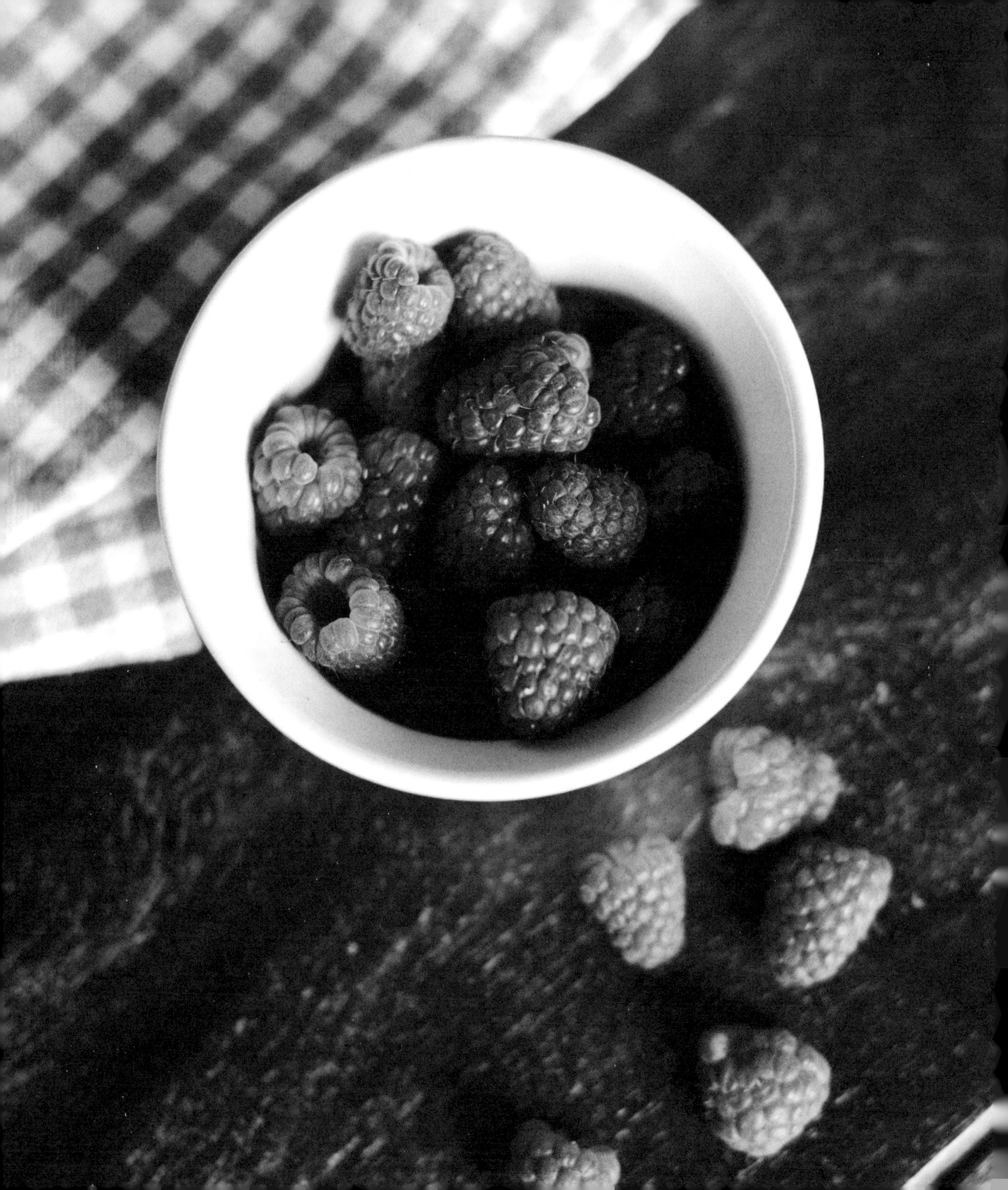

The Hospitality Code

Some people don't send invitations the week before. The woman with the kind eyes and gentle smile didn't. She just called and asked if we wanted to share an evening meal. No proper etiquette rules governed the gathering that was about to take place.

We brought what we had, and she offered the same—*what she had.*

She welcomed us in through the back kitchen door, light spilling through and guests spilling in, the oak table filled up with the place settings and the counters filled up with the preparation. I remember the sweet yellow corn being husked, the white linen cloth with the navy trim covering the rolls. Someone was stirring lemonade.

She was joy overflowing, arms wide open, laughter and welcome and love. The evening was magic, brimming with the contentment of sweet friendship and good food.

It is the only dinner gathering I remember from my youth. I have never forgotten how everything was awash with light and welcome and love.

Some people live a life filled with welcome.

I want to be one of them.

From the beginning of time, God sought to teach His people how to welcome. "Thou shalt not oppress a stranger: for ye know the heart of a stranger, seeing ye were strangers in the land of Egypt" (Exodus 23:9). It's a simple verse hidden in a chapter that lays out the law of godly conduct. *You will know how to love the sojourners because you have been an outcast yourself. Your heart understands the need for inclusion, for gathering in. You understand because you have felt unwanted before.*

It was a law of hospitality, a code, defined in the pages of Old Testament scripture: *Never allow someone to feel unwelcome.* It was Abraham welcoming strangers after a long journey (see Genesis 18). It was a woman drawing water for a stranger at the well (see Genesis 24). It was the preparing of a bed and a candlestick and a table for a prophet who continually passed by (see 2 Kings 4:8–10). These stories are the living out of the hospitality code.

Jesus taught of it again in the New Testament: "For I was an hungred, and ye gave me meat: I was thirsty, and ye gave me drink: I was a stranger, and ye took me in" (Matthew 25:35). Hospitality is a higher way of living. It's having the eyes to see someone as they are and to look for and give what they lack. It's not offering a coat to someone who is thirsty; Jesus taught that if someone is hungry, we should meet them in their hunger.

The hospitality code is as simple as this: Look at the heart. Assess the need. Offer what you have. Always.

The law of hospitality appears again in the book of Hebrews. "*Let . . . love continue*," we are counseled. "Be not forgetful to entertain strangers: for thereby some have entertained angels unawares" (Hebrews 13:1–2; emphasis added). Perhaps it is in the loving that strangers become friends. Through love we see what might otherwise have been concealed: the makings of a sweet, unexpected relationship.

Hospitality is a promise. A blessing. When we understand the hospitality code, we enter into the ministry of heaven.

Hospitality is the art of **visualizing the need**

Hospitality is the art of **offering what we have**

Hospitality is the art of **entertaining angels**

Hospitality is the **welcoming in**

BE . . . GIVEN TO HOSPITALITY.

Romans 12:10, 13

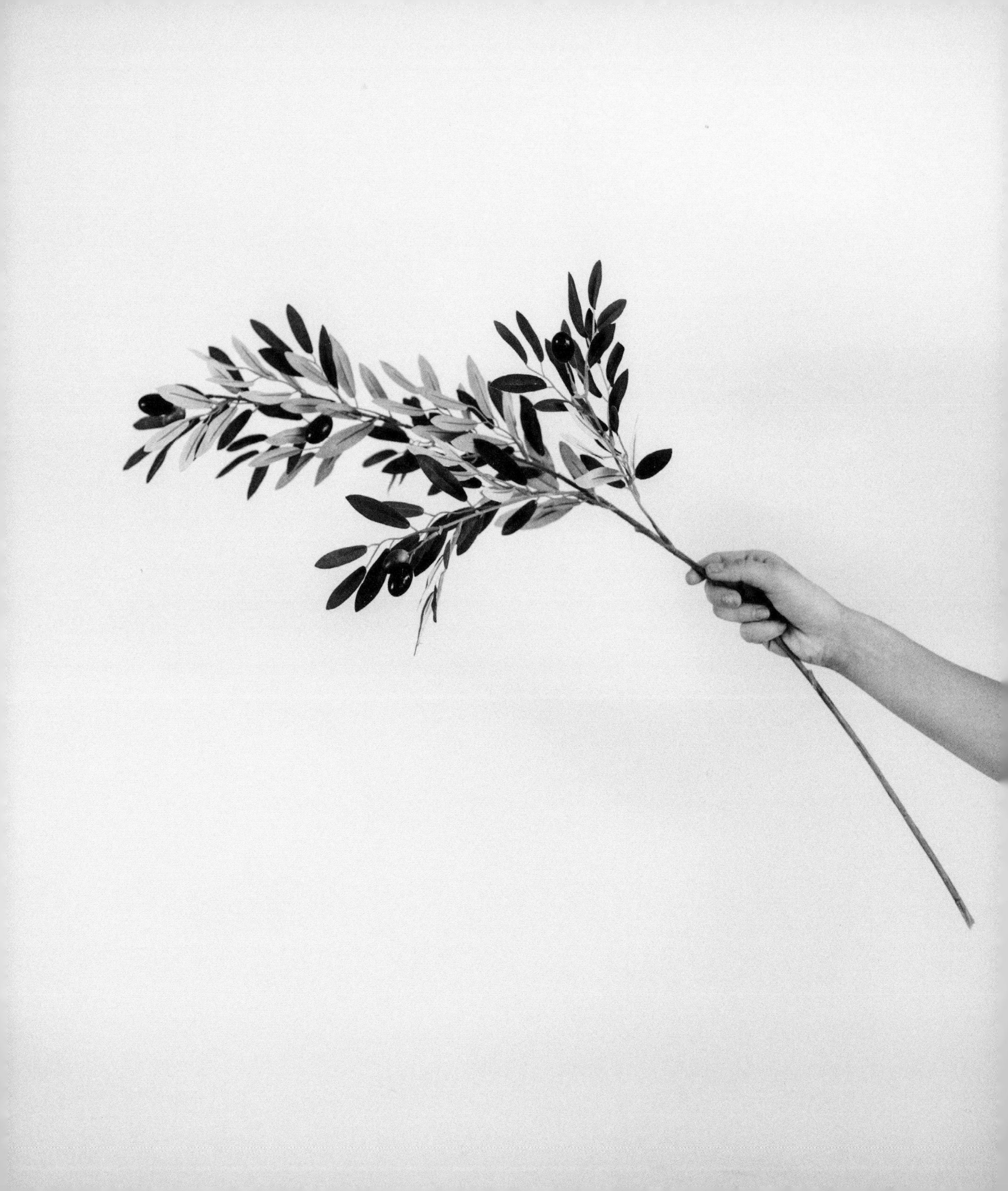

An Offering

After the rain stopped, Noah opened up the window of the place that had become a refuge, a shelter from the storm, a sanctuary of faith. He sent out a dove to see if the earth had dried.

"But the dove found no rest for the sole of her foot," and she returned, and he "pulled her in unto him." Into the refuge. Into the sanctuary of faith. He waited seven more days, and in the early morning light, Noah sent her off again. This time, when she returned to the refuge, she came with an olive leaf, and Noah knew the earth would soon be hospitable again. After the next seven days, when Noah sent her out once again, the dove was welcomed into the world that had been healed, and when she did not return, Noah knew it was safe to gather his family onto the land (Genesis 8:9–12). For Noah and his family, the olive leaf was a sign of peace, celebration, hospitality, and life.

As I read this story, I am most interested in the gopher-wood ark that became a refuge, a shelter from the storm, a sanctuary of faith. My heart is caught up in it because of the call of a prophet today—a prophet who warns that the "assaults of the adversary are increasing exponentially, in intensity and in variety."

I consider the father who watched for the dove at the window, who pulled her in unto him, into the refuge he had built with his own hands in preparation for the storm that would come. I hear the echo of a prophet today inviting each of us to conscientiously and carefully transform our home into a sanctuary of faith, to incorporate changes that would be "dramatic and sustaining," to create a haven that would protect from the adversary's influence. A shelter from the storm. A refuge.

In Noah's day, the sign of the olive leaf was a welcome back into the world. In our day, perhaps the olive leaf becomes a symbol of gathering into the home for peace, for celebration, for hospitality, and for life.

Ours is a God who loves creating places of refuge, who designs shelters for gathering in.

It was September, and I walked the streets of Nauvoo at twilight. My steps were drawn to the house down by the water. I stood next to the foundation and touched the mortar with the tip of my finger, and a familiar verse came to mind: "And it shall be for a house for boarding, a house that strangers may come from afar to lodge therein; therefore let it be a good house, worthy of all acceptation, that the weary traveler may find health and safety while he shall contemplate the word of the Lord. . . . It shall be holy" (Doctrine and Covenants 124:23–24). The Lord named this house: "And let the name of that house be called Nauvoo House; and let it be a delightful habitation for man, and a resting-place for the weary traveler, . . . that he may receive also the counsel from those whom I have set to be as plants of renown, and as watchmen upon her walls" (Doctrine and Covenants 124:60–61).

There are so many things I love about the Nauvoo House. First, it was built for a people who knew what it was like to be cast out, what it meant to feel unwelcome. This would become a house of hospitality, a good house, and everyone would be welcome there. Surely the front porch, with its welcome mat and open door, would whisper the invitation *Come and stay*. The home was meant to offer moments of delight as well as conversations filled with scripture and God's goodness. The counsel given within those four walls would include fruits of wisdom and the safety of watchcare. Maybe the understanding of what it was to feel unwelcome inspired the building of a home that would create welcome. That need to create welcome is found in us as well. It is our story. The Nauvoo House represents everything I pray for in a home. I love the promises there.

Lord, fill my house with hospitality, goodness, welcome, refuge, God's word, and love.

Let it be holy.

※

It was September of 2011, and my daughters and I were driving in the car. Fall hung rich with color on the trees; school had begun. I had recently read the verses about the Nauvoo House and wondered if the passage might become our family scripture for the school year. We had never had a family scripture before, but it seemed like a good idea, so I asked the girls what they thought.

My vision for the year included the girls inviting their friends home for lunch and entertaining crowds of teenagers on the weekends. I planned to stock the pantry full of brownies and fun drinks, and ours would become a home where people loved to gather. They could play Ping-Pong in the basement, enjoy pickleball outside, and listen to music as they made treats in the kitchen. The girls were all in.

I should give a word of caution here about choosing a theme scripture for the year. You just don't know what might happen.

In October, I was in Portland to speak at an event when my daughter Meg called me. There was a boy at the door—Ian—one of the boys my husband, Greg, coached. Ian wanted to turn his life around, start going to church, and serve a mission. He wanted to know if he could move in with us for a time. So Meg asked if she could let him stay in the bedroom upstairs because no one was currently using it.

I told her that was fine.

In December, Greg's sister called. Things were rough at home; it had been that way for years, but now it was finally time to move on. She wondered if she and the kids might move in for a little while. Just until she got her feet back under her.

I bought bunk beds from the classified ads, and we moved our two girls up to the piano room. I purchased metal clothing rods from Walmart and found an accordion divider online to put in the archway to give them more privacy. Greg's sister and family moved into the girls' room downstairs.

In January, our son Josh came home from his mission; a few months later, our son Garett also came home from his mission; and in the spring, our other son, Caleb, moved home from college. We had already put three beds in the bedroom upstairs, and there wasn't any room for Caleb. So I put a mattress under the Ping-Pong table downstairs.

I remember praying one night, asking God what He wanted me to do. We didn't have any more room, we didn't have any more money, we were bursting at the seams of this house, and no one was going to be playing Ping-Pong anytime soon. *Is the Ping-Pong table more important than the boy upstairs preparing for a mission, the sister going through a divorce, the boys figuring out how to move forward, or the girls in the piano room?* Then the Spirit whispered a promise: *You provide the room; I will provide the means.*

And God did.

When I look back at that time, I don't remember the laundry or the shopping or the finances. I remember two things—the kids coming over at noon for turkey and Swiss cheese sandwiches with avocado, and the many people gathered with us at 9:45 every evening for scripture study and sweet conversations about the Lord.

I can't tell you how many sandwiches I made that year or how many conversations we had that centered on the word of the Lord. I just remember everyone piled into the family room at night in front of the fireplace, squished on the couches and snuggled up in blankets on the floor. I remember the conversations.

Weary travelers showed up on our porch, and we offered an olive leaf. We pulled them into us. Into the refuge. Into the sanctuary of faith. Into the gathering home.

AND IT SHALL BE FOR A HOUSE FOR BOARDING,

A HOUSE THAT STRANGERS MAY COME FROM AFAR TO

LODGE THEREIN; THEREFORE LET IT BE A GOOD HOUSE,

WORTHY OF ALL ACCEPTATION, THAT THE WEARY TRAVELER

MAY FIND HEALTH AND SAFETY WHILE HE SHALL CONTEMPLATE

THE WORD OF THE LORD. . . . IT SHALL BE HOLY.

Doctrine and Covenants 124:23–24

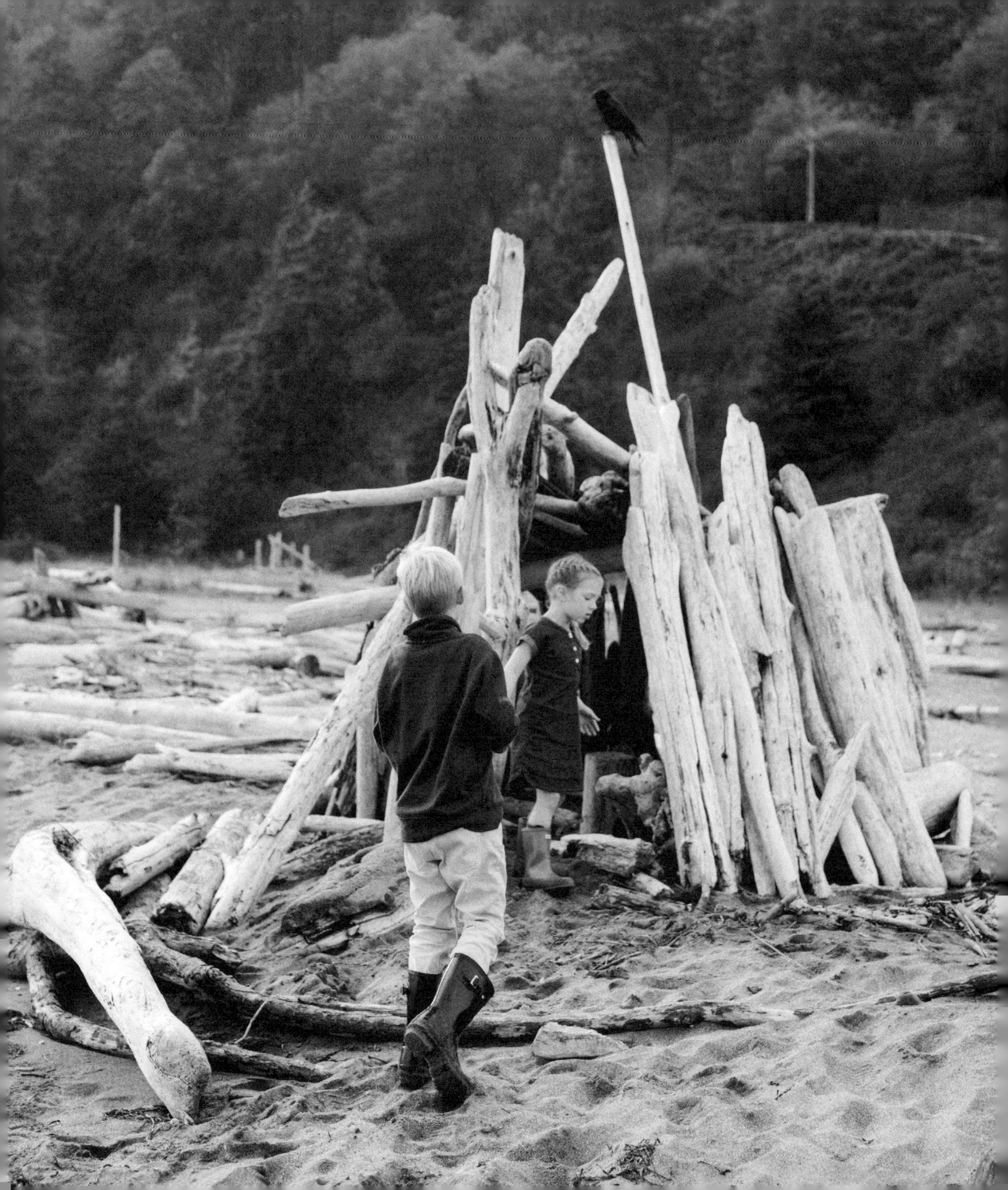

Building the Refuge

My friend was supposed to be focusing on the meeting taking place, but his thoughts were caught up on the painting hanging in the high council room. He just didn't love it. *Why do we have this painting?* he wondered to himself. *There are beautiful paintings of finished temples. Why did someone choose to hang a painting of an unfinished temple here?*

Walter Rane's painting of the Kirtland Temple under construction is messy with detail. Half of the temple has been plastered white, but the bottom layer is still red brick. Scaffolding has been placed around one whole side of the temple, and a man stands at the top of a ladder, laying more plaster. There is a fire burning in the middle of the painting, with dirty smoke rising to the sky. Two men are mixing water and fine sand in a crudely made form. There are piles of dirt, an unattended wagon, and barrels of water placed haphazardly around the yard. Everyone in the painting is working except one young mother wearing a green cloak, standing next to her tiny daughter. This woman has paused from her errand to watch the building that is taking place.

As my friend sat staring at the painting, the Spirit whispered, *This is a painting of you. You are an unfinished temple that I am still constructing.*

It was true of him, my stake president, and of every person who would walk through the door of his office during the tenure of his calling. It is true of each of us. I have loved that painting ever since I heard his story. The Lord is in the process of building each of us.

I can't help but consider the mother in the green cloak, so intent on watching the process of building. I think of my own home and realize I am that woman. When I look at what is taking place within my four walls, everything is messy with detail. Some things are haphazard, unattended, unfinished. We are a work in progress. But no one has given up.

Unfinished doesn't equate to failure.

Instead it is a sign that He isn't through building us yet. There is beauty ahead. I know there is because I have seen the completed temple that was being built in that Walter Rane painting. I have walked through the doors of that beautifully finished house in Kirtland. I have sat in the pews, and I have felt the peace.

That beauty is what I wish for my own home when all is said and done.

But today I am the woman in the green cloak, intent on watching the workings of it all. The woman who has paused from her errand to consider.

I listened carefully as my good friend shared her advice about creating a protected day. "Set aside one day for saying no," she told me with conviction. "It will change your life."

"I don't understand," I said. "I am desperate for something like that, and I am wondering how you really make it work."

"It's my day," she replied simply. "Blocked. I don't say yes to anything. Instead, I meet with Jesus, and then I just do what I want. I can sleep, read, walk, meet up with a friend. I feel like I got my life back!"

A consecrated day. A pause from the errand. A moment to consider.

I decided to set aside Wednesdays as my consecrated day. I leave Wednesday evenings completely free and set aside a few hours during the day to meet with Jesus. I pull out paper, and I ask for heaven's help as I consider all the things that are my unfinished work—my relationships, my home, my scripture teaching, my family's mealtimes, and our Sabbath moments. The messiness of my life.

This is my pause—the time I set aside my work to look closely at what I am building. Those Wednesday pauses give me my life back.

Perhaps you would like to take a pause—to step back from your errands, to consider your unfinished work. Maybe you don't have an entire day to set aside, but perhaps you will set aside a few hours each week to consider three areas of intention for your gathering home: creating the space, gathering the people, and giving your love.

CREATE THE SPACE

I am in love with the first five words of the Torah, "When God began to create . . ." Creating is innate in us; it is woven throughout the fabric of life. Every important moment begins as an idea. There is a time of creation, of dreaming, of wishing and vision. Creating is what makes the magic that becomes the root of memory.

What does creating look like?

When I said yes to the speaking engagement in Murrieta, California, I didn't know about the four deadlines I would be writing toward that same weekend. I was overwhelmed with the work and the weight of it all. A friend reached out and asked what I wanted to do to fill up the hours the day before I spoke. I told her I had to write. "Come write in my backyard," she said. "It is quiet there." I took her up on the offer.

When I arrived, she opened the sliding glass door and welcomed me into her backyard. "I spent the last couple of days getting ready for you," she said with a smile. "We cleaned things up from the winter, trimmed the plants. I even invited the birds back." I laughed at that, but when I looked, I could see birds in the feeders, on the branches, and in the bath. Everyone was welcome there. I wrote for hours in that haven, soft sun on my back, birds in the trees. This kind woman had intentionally created a sanctuary in my behalf.

The prophet has asked each of us to do the same—create a sanctuary. A place for gathering. A refuge. What will yours look like? What will you create?

The secret to creating a refuge is filling a place with love and security. The art of hospitality is creating a feeling of welcome in everything that happens under our roof with the people who enter through the same door and eat the same meals and sweep the same floor. These are our people. What type of sanctuary are we creating for them?

The first step of creating a gathering home is to invite the birds back.

Begin to create.

GATHER THE PEOPLE

A gathering is nothing without the people. The light and life of the coming together is kindled by the hearts that gather.

But what if they won't come?

Here's something important to know: The secret of the gathering is meeting people where they are.

In the days before church was home centered, when Monday nights were sacred and reserved for evenings at home, one father struggled to gather his teenagers for a Monday-evening lesson. There were angry words and tension. *How much longer?* There was the counting down until they didn't have to sit in the same room, doing the same thing, when none of their friends were doing this.

Then one Monday night, the father stopped and picked up a pie on his way home from work. After the dinner was over and the dishes were done, at just about the time he should have been calling for everyone to come to the family room, he didn't. Instead he pulled one small plate out of the cupboard. He sat down at the kitchen table without saying a word and cut himself a slice of pie. After he had taken a couple of bites, one of the kids noticed what he was doing. "Can I have a piece?"

Before long, every member of the family was sitting around the table eating a piece of pie. "I've been thinking today about something important," the father said, casually bringing up the subject he would have normally taught in the family room amidst the tension and the counting down and the angry words.

They talked for half an hour while they ate pie. And no one noticed that they had just spent a Monday evening at home talking about spiritual things. It was dessert with Dad—that's all.

Somehow that wise father had figured out how to create magic and gather souls—how to meet his teenage kids where they were.

The magic was in a simple invitation: Come to the table.

Consider a mind shift. Instead of simply focusing on the purpose of the gathering, maybe you could focus first on the people and where they are. As you go through the creating process, keep in mind the needs of the people you are gathering. Where are their hearts and minds? What do they need?

Sometimes we are so quick to turn to scripture and lengthy conversations and gospel doctrine that we may forget how well Jesus simply loved. The Spirit will whisper to your heart during your consecrated moments. He will inspire you to know how to meet your people right where they are. As you fill out the pages in your Planning Pages section each week, don't forget to write the names of people. As you plan out your gatherings for this year, consider all the people who fill your life. Ponder them individually. Do something different. Meet them where they are.

Stop and pick up a pie.

GIVE YOUR LOVE

Finally, there is the giving.

Giving, in its best form, comes from a place of vulnerability. It doesn't require perfection, a clean house, or your best china. Giving is grace without apology. It is the understanding that you can't meet people as they are if you can't show up as you are.

What do you have to give?

Giving is stopping a project that you had set aside your Saturday afternoon for in order to sit on the couch and listen. Giving is delivering a batch of cookies. Giving is stooping down to the level of a toddler to hear about the child's best stuffed dog. Giving is making someone their favorite soup. Giving is time. It is showing others their importance in your life by stopping everything else when they arrive.

Don't get me wrong. Sometimes giving *is* setting a beautiful table that lets people know you spent time preparing for a gathering with them. But we mustn't forget that giving is also pushing pause on the mess to set aside a moment for the individual.

Giving is relationship building and strengthening and focusing.

Giving is love.

This is an invitation to set aside a consecrated moment every week to build your refuge. To pause from your errand to consider your work. To spend a few hours with Jesus. To plan.

How will you create, gather, and give?

Create,

Gather,

and Give

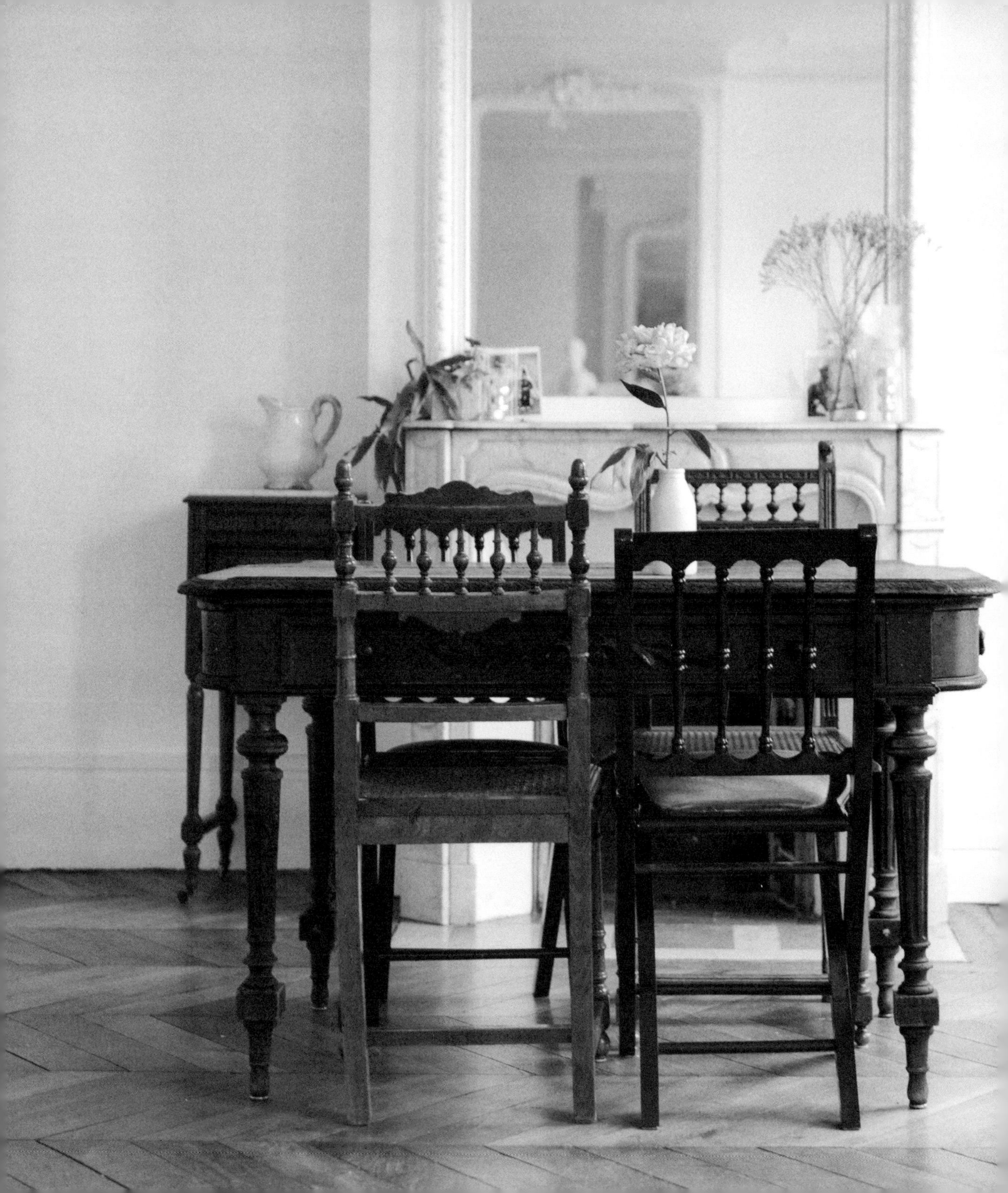

PART ONE

THE
SACRED
IN THE
EVERYDAY

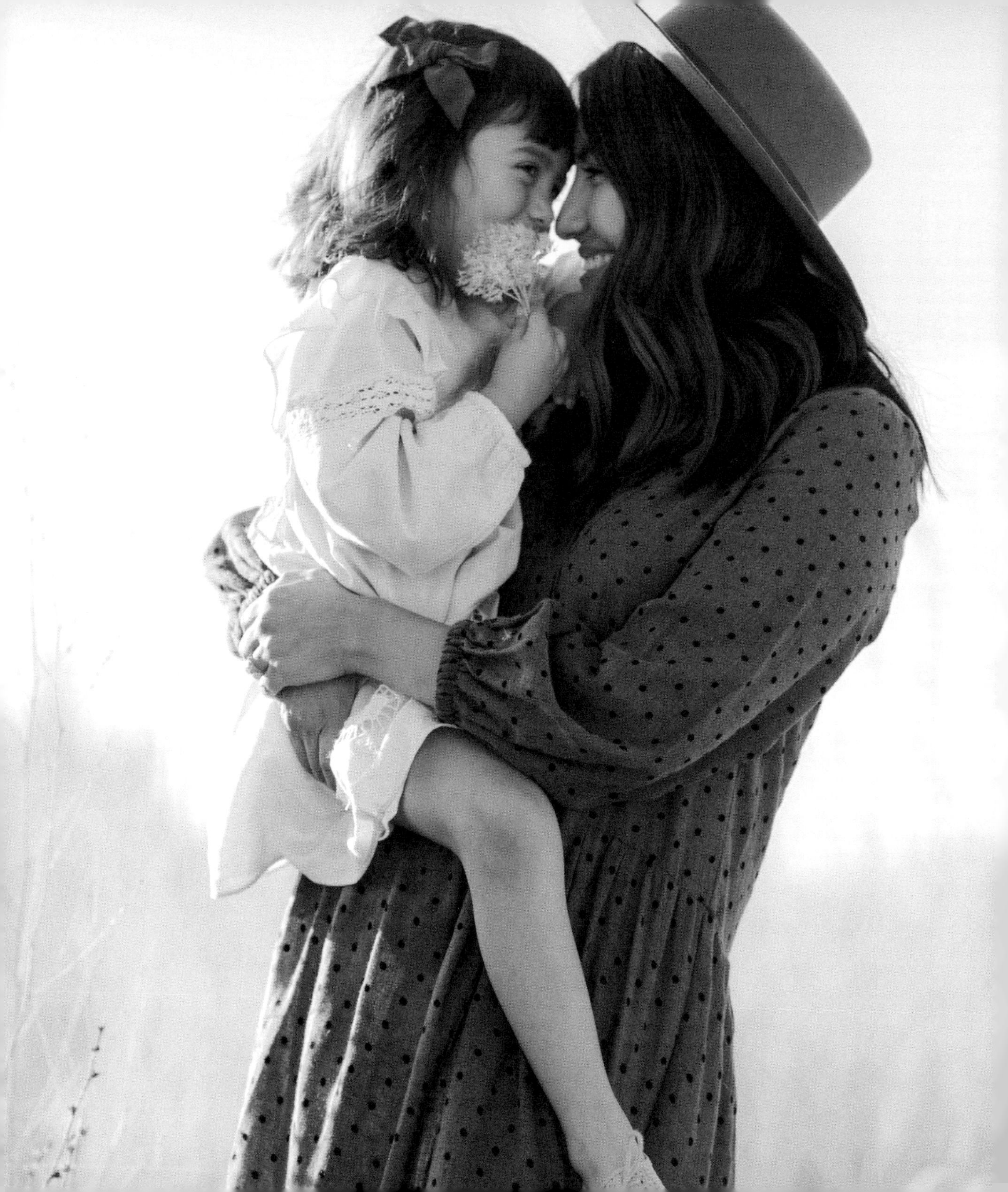

CELEBRATING THE SACRED IN THE EVERYDAY

When winter gives way to spring, I feel hope. As spring settles into summer, my heart feels its most content. As the late August nights begin to fill with the crispness of fall, I long for the refuge inside my home. And when the first winter flakes fall, I find myself drawn to warmth and light. Before I know it, hope is stirring, and my heart starts watching for spring to make its entrance once again.

There is a rhythm within the ebb and flow of the seasons. For some reason, it steadies my heart. There is growth and change and settling and comfort. My soul responds to the routine. Perhaps that is why the Lord fills up our every day with sacred rhythms. We pause for prayer, we rest on the Sabbaths, we gather for mealtime, for scripture, for rites of passage, and for celebrations. There is an ebb and flow to our lives.

The idea of the "gathering home" is meant to help us intentionally embrace these sacred rhythms with the understanding that lives will change, that seasons will come and go. Over time, from year to year, things will look different. People may move in and out of our homes. Our neighborhoods may change. Single adults may get married. Littles will become teenagers. Teenagers will become adults. Before we know it, our gathering home could be filled with grandchildren. Every now and again, we should give space for becoming deliberate about the celebrations and the sacredness in this season of life we are in, whatever it looks like now.

When was the last time you focused on your everyday gatherings, your weekly rhythms, your celebrations? On the pages ahead, we provide ideas for you to begin the process of creating, gathering, and giving, of remodeling your home, of building your sanctuary of faith. The planning pages for this section can be found on page 119. May the Lord bless you in your efforts.

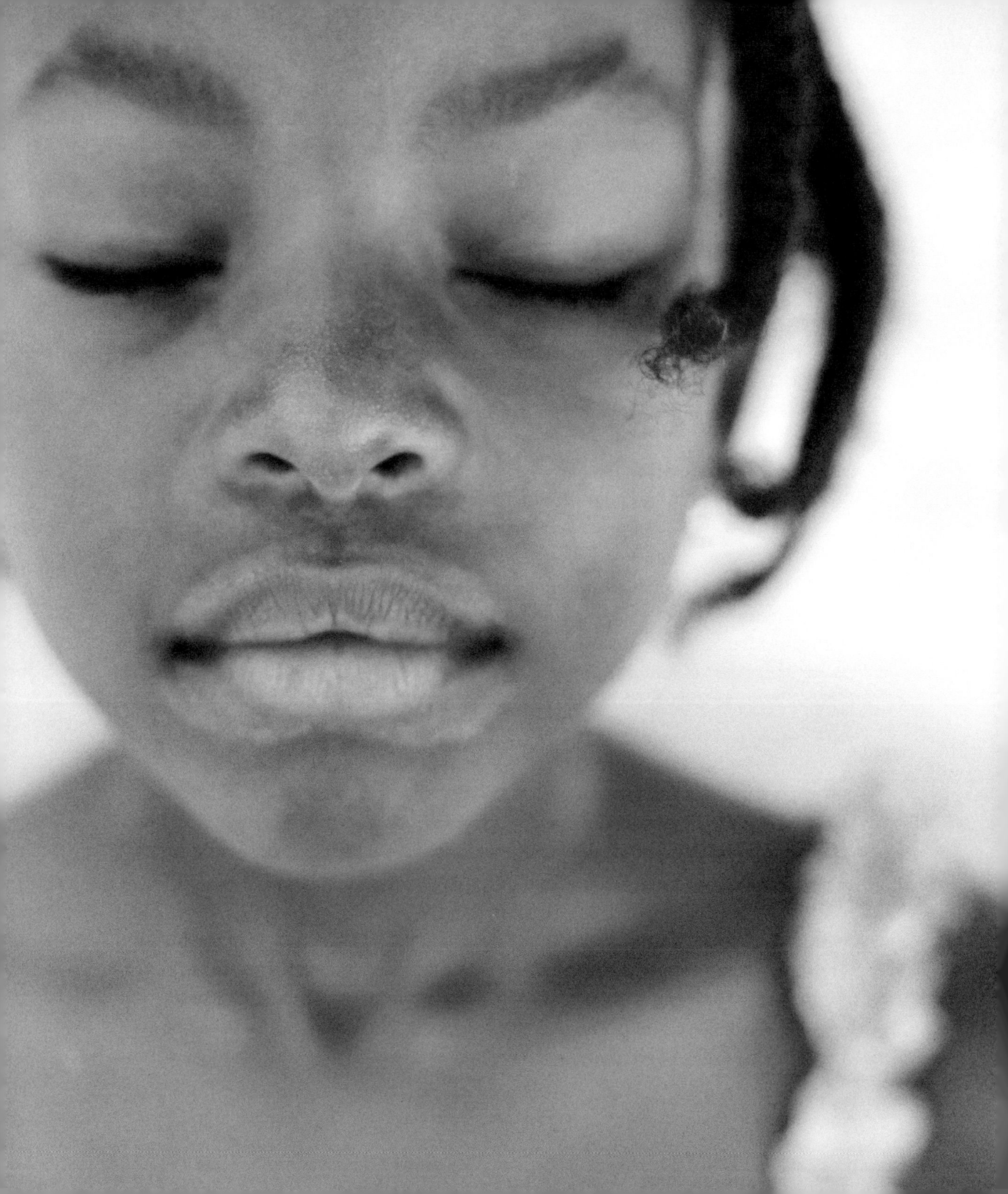

> I REMEMBER MY MOTHER'S PRAYERS AND THEY HAVE ALWAYS FOLLOWED ME.
> THEY HAVE CLUNG TO ME ALL MY LIFE.
>
> *Abraham Lincoln*

Prayer

When the hard things happen, I always make one phone call.

Light the prayer candle.

It's the first thing I say to my dear friend when our family is in need of her prayers, because I know just what she will do. As soon as I tell her the trial, she will walk over to the cupboard where she keeps her prayer candle, and she will pull it down from the shelf. The candle will stay in the middle of her kitchen counter, all lit up with the reminder of the need pressing down hard in my home. Every time she walks past that candle, she will offer a silent prayer in our behalf. It is her reminder of the need for heaven's help in my home. In times of trouble, that flame stays on constantly so that we are kept present in her thoughts and prayers throughout the day. And it's not just for our family—it is a part of her faith tradition to light the candle for everyone who needs her prayers. Some months she lights it almost every day, and because of that, her kids have come to know exactly what it is. As soon as they see the prayer candle with its dancing flame on the counter, they ask who she is praying for.

The symbol of a candle has often been used to signify the importance of relationships. Some mothers light a candle in their home when a child is deployed and burn it every day until their child returns. It was a tradition in Old Nauvoo to light a candle in the window if you were accepting visitors on certain evenings. For my friend, a lighted candle represents the keeping of someone close in her thoughts and in her prayers.

Whether it is a prayer candle, or a prayer list, or a journal filled with names and written prayers by your bed, perhaps you could find a tangible way to remember the people you love in your prayers. Your symbol could become a witness of the power of prayer taking place within the walls of your home.

What ways have you found to bring the power of prayer into your life?

When the children were little, prayer was a whisper in their ears—with their arms folded tight and eyes squished shut—just before tucking them in with a soft blanket at dusk. As they grew older, prayer was heads bowed before the meal or at the close of scripture reading or before a long road trip in the car. As time went on, prayer was gathering with one another in unexpected moments to petition the Lord for the one who was sick, the one who was hurting, the one who needed heaven's help. In our home now, prayer is circling around for the beginning of miracles and coming together again for the giving of thanks.

Prayer is the connection point. It's where we meet with hands clasped, heads bowed, and hearts heavenward.

Over time, prayer can become the rhythm, the breathing in and exhaling out, of a home. The sunrise and the sunset of the pressing needs. The time taken to ask each individual what words you can offer in their behalf every morning and every evening and when morning comes again. It's inviting Heavenly Father into your home, into your struggles, into the conversation of your life.

Now my little ones are grown. I pray alone on most days, but my prayers are filled with them, and it warms my heart to know their prayers are filled with each other. Because we don't live together, we communicate our needs to each other by text. Short messages send people to their knees: *I'm taking a test at 10:00 a.m. . . . I have an important meeting at work. . . . We received bad news about the pregnancy. . . . I'm struggling with some things. . . . Can you pray?* The two most frequently used emojis in our family texts are the laughing face and the prayer hands. They have become symbols of the most important things we do in our family: laugh and pray.

What if prayer was interwoven into the fabric of our homes?

What if it became the mainstay?

I have learned that a prayer request written down is a prayer remembered. Because of that, there is a space for prayer requests on each of the weekly planning pages at the end of this book. A space for contemplation each week.

Let me give an example of how you might use the Prayer section on your weekly pages: A dear friend of mine sits down to ponder at the beginning of every week. Her system is different from most people's. Instead of setting weekly physical, spiritual, or mental goals, she chooses goals based on relationships. She asks herself: *What do I need to do this week as a daughter of God? What do I need to do this week as a wife? As a mother? As a sister? As a daughter? What do I need to do as a ministering sister? As a friend? What prayers should I pray? What service can I give?* She records her thoughts on her planning pages. Every goal is driven by what she can offer to a relationship, both in service and in prayer. Perhaps you would like to try something similar.

Prayer

AS A . . .	WHO OR WHAT ARE YOU **PRAYING** FOR?
mother	for Caleb and Maria to feel welcome in their new neighborhood
friend	for Kris to find great joy
sister	gratitude for Lu

How will you make prayer an intentional part of your gathering home?

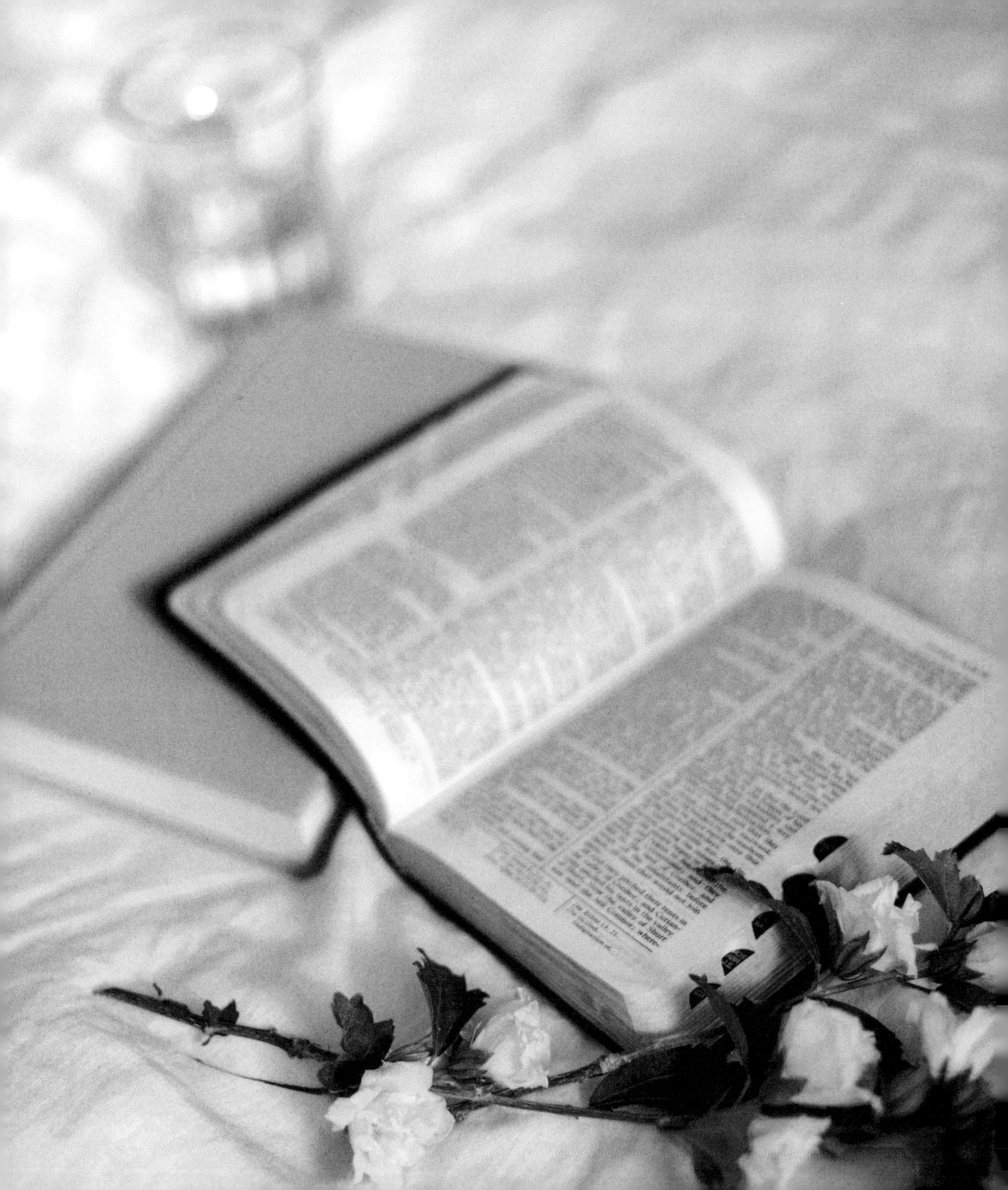

HE WHO READS IT OFTENEST WILL LIKE IT BEST.

Joseph Smith

Scripture

Throughout time, prophets have spoken of the blessings that come from scripture. In our generation it is the same. Prophetic blessings attributed to scripture reading include the promise of power, of an added measure of the Spirit that will permeate our homes. An increase of love, of reverence, of respect. Reading scripture will become a precursor of strength, testimony, insight, and conviction. Scripture is a source of drawing nearer to God. Hearts being lifted. There will be an added measure of spirituality, fortification, peace, joy, and happiness. These are the prophetic blessings promised to those who read the familiar words on holy pages, the book of evidences, the verses of scripture.

The blessings that come through scripture study can permeate relationships of any type, whether we are studying individually or with a family or a congregation. What are the ways you gather for scripture study?

Perhaps you study alone most days, and with your church community once a week. Companionship comes as you invite the Spirit to permeate your home, as you draw nearer to God, as your relationship with Jesus Christ increases. You might look for solutions for friends or children as you read and send them a letter or a text with your discoveries. For gathering to happen, people don't have to be present. Relationships can be strengthened as you read with loved ones in mind.

Maybe you study with a spouse. Have your tried taking a question into your studies each day? Do you share discoveries from your personal study time? Have you ever stumbled on something that wasn't clear and invited your companion to be part of your search for understanding?

What if my children are little? you ask. Consider purchasing an inexpensive set of scriptures and a box of colored pencils for each child, and let them color those pages full as you read aloud. Through the process, their minds will become familiar with the rhythm of sacred words day after day. Perhaps they will repeat the important phrases after you, again, and one more time. Or you might bring out the illustrated scriptures, tell them the stories in your own words, say the names of the heroes until they become familiar.

As they grow a little older? Try to spend as much time answering their questions as you do reading the verses. Ask questions of your own. Teach them to understand the culture and the context of the stories. Look up words. Follow footnotes. If you are reading a parable, perhaps you can have them draw the story. If it is a description of Christ, you might take time to mark each word. If there is a "power phrase," write it out and consider memorizing it as a family. Look for scriptures promising protection or divine aid or other needed blessings, and keep lists on the blank pages at the back of your book of scripture. Discover the Bible Dictionary, and the Guide to the Scriptures, and the Topical Guide. Try to look for the application, for what makes a scripture important in everyday life. Falling in love with scripture comes with time and positive experience.

In their teenage years? These are the critical years, the years when you wonder how to gather them there and why reading scripture together has gotten so hard. Consider having separate study for the littles and the bigs. Your job for the older ones might take a shift, from teacher to guide. Learning to read the scriptures on their own is becoming a crucial skill, one that will carry them through life. Consider setting a fifteen-minute timer. Choose one chapter to read. Have everyone read in silence on their own for the fifteen minutes. As they read, you might invite them each to find the one verse that is most important in their life on that day. Just one verse. *Their verse.* When the timer goes off, stop reading even if you haven't reached the end of the chapter. Ask each person in the room to share their favorite verse and tell why they chose it. Over time, they will begin to realize how the Spirit speaks to them, in their own language, about the conditions and particulars of their own lives. They will learn how to read scripture on their own.

The important thing isn't what time of day you read; the important thing is that you do it. Set aside an amount of time that works for you and your situation, for your family and their ages, and let scripture reading become the pattern of your every day. There was a time when we would listen to scripture in the mornings as I drove carpool to school. We would push *pause* on the important parts and discuss what we were learning. Then there were the years when I read aloud to our family over breakfast in the morning.

My favorite was when everyone was older. The call for scriptures was at 9:45 p.m. We read together until 10:00 p.m. Sometimes friends would read with us. Whoever was in the house was invited. After reading, we went around the room, and each person shared one favorite verse. After we had gathered for prayer, we put the house to bed. The kitchen was closed, the lights were turned off, each of us made our way to our own rooms, and the Spirit was strong, and the protection was sure, and we climbed into bed with our hearts drawn nearer to God. Those were the sweetest days.

Take time to fill out your family scripture goals. The weekly planning pages at the end of this book include a section to help you be more intentional about your scripture study. A filled-out section might look something like this:

Scripture

WHAT QUESTION WILL YOU TAKE TO THE SCRIPTURES?
How can we have more peace?

FAMILY **PROTECTION** SCRIPTURE:
Isaiah 32:17-18

How will you make scripture an intentional part of your gathering home?

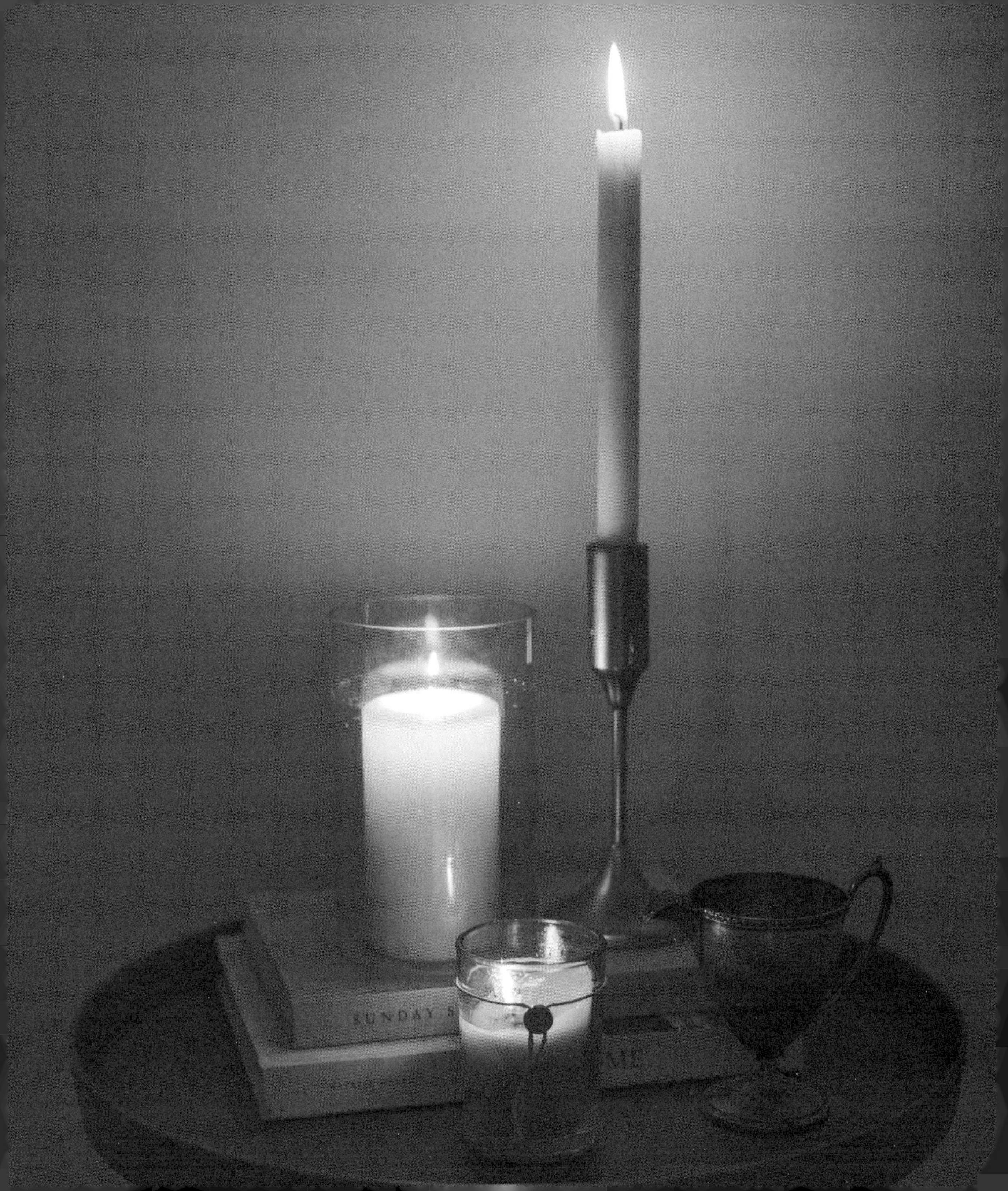
SUNDAY S

A WORLD WITHOUT A SABBATH WOULD BE . . . LIKE A SUMMER WITHOUT FLOWERS.

Henry Ward Beecher

The Sabbath

Shabbat shalom. It is said as a greeting, and if you are Jewish, on the day before the Sabbath, *Shabbat shalom* is your wish for an upcoming day of peace. It is what I wish for too: a day of peace.

I watch her walk over to the table with the white candles waiting there. The sun is setting, and the lighting of the candles on Sabbath eve is the welcoming in of harmony in the home and the invitation for Sabbath joy. Eighteen minutes before sunset, the two Sabbath candles are lit, representing the first words of the Sabbath commandments. One means *to keep*, and the other, *to remember*. The woman bends low and kindles the flame, then draws her hands around the candles and toward her face three times—drawing the light inside, allowing the light of Shabbat to fill the room and surround each person, inviting rest.

This ritual is the rhythm of a Jewish home, the rite of a mother to welcome in resting and keeping and remembering. It is the preparing of the home and heart.

How do you keep and remember the Sabbath?

It entered my heart with great urgency, this need to separate the Sabbath from the everyday, the ordinary routine, the getting things done, the lists and the laundry and all the usual things. "How can you ensure that your behavior on the Sabbath will lead to joy and rejoicing?" President Russell M. Nelson asked. "In addition to your going to church, partaking of the sacrament, and being diligent in your specific call to serve, what other activities would help to make the Sabbath a delight for you? What sign will you give to the Lord to show your love for Him?"

What would make this holy day different from a typical day?

Immediately my thoughts filled with Christmas: a holy day, different from the mundane. *And why is it?* It wasn't long before I knew the why. I felt it settle in my heart first, the knowledge that it's the preparing, the creating, the gathering, the giving. It's the change in the music we listen to, the anticipation of special meals we rarely eat. It's treasured traditions that we anticipate, reserved specifically for that season. It's pajamas, and stockings hung, and carols, and our favorite Christmas cookies, and Jesus. These are all of the reasons we gather.

These are the memories that mark how we *keep* and *remember* Christmas.

I realized the Sabbath is a holy day much like Christmas is. What if I were to enter into the preparing, the creating, the gathering, the giving, in the very same way? The change in the music we listen to, the foods reserved for special days, the things to look forward to that happen only on Sundays. Could it be done? Could we start looking forward to Sundays the same way we anticipate Christmas?

I gathered the family together for a council. "Tell me your favorite songs about Jesus," I invited. "What activities would you love to do together as a family that we don't have time for during the week?" *Taking a walk. Baking cookies. Playing games together next to the fire. Watching an uplifting movie. Sitting on the lawn in the shade of a summer afternoon.* Maybe the things that bond us could fill up our Sabbath days. We could reserve those moments for being together in celebration. Could it be that the *keeping* of the Sabbath was meant for the keeping of each other? Of turning hearts to family and to God? Of *remembering* the most important things?

On Christmas, we read Luke 2. We turn to scripture that has become familiar to us, those first words that hint of the celebration ahead: "And it came to pass in those days, that there went out a decree from Caesar Augustus" (Luke 2:1). And now the prophet calls for us to make the words of scripture familiar on our Sabbaths, too. To gather for home-centered learning. To create space for the teaching of His word. If you do, "changes in your family will be dramatic and sustaining," he promises. "The influence of the adversary in *your* life and in *your* home will decrease." Each one of us is to transform our home "into a sanctuary of faith," he counsels, "conscientiously and carefully." Then, our "Sabbath days will truly be a delight."

What will this look like for your family?

Take time to fill out your Sabbath goals in the planning sheets at the end of this book. The section for the Sabbath day might look something like this:

Sabbath

HOW WILL YOU **KEEP** THE SABBATH THIS WEEK?	HOW WILL YOU **REMEMBER** GOD & OTHERS?	HOW CAN YOU CREATE MOMENTS OF TRADITION?
I will spend time intentionally preparing for the sacrament	Go visit Grandma & Grandpa	Make chocolate chip cookies

How will you make each Sabbath an intentional part of your gathering home?

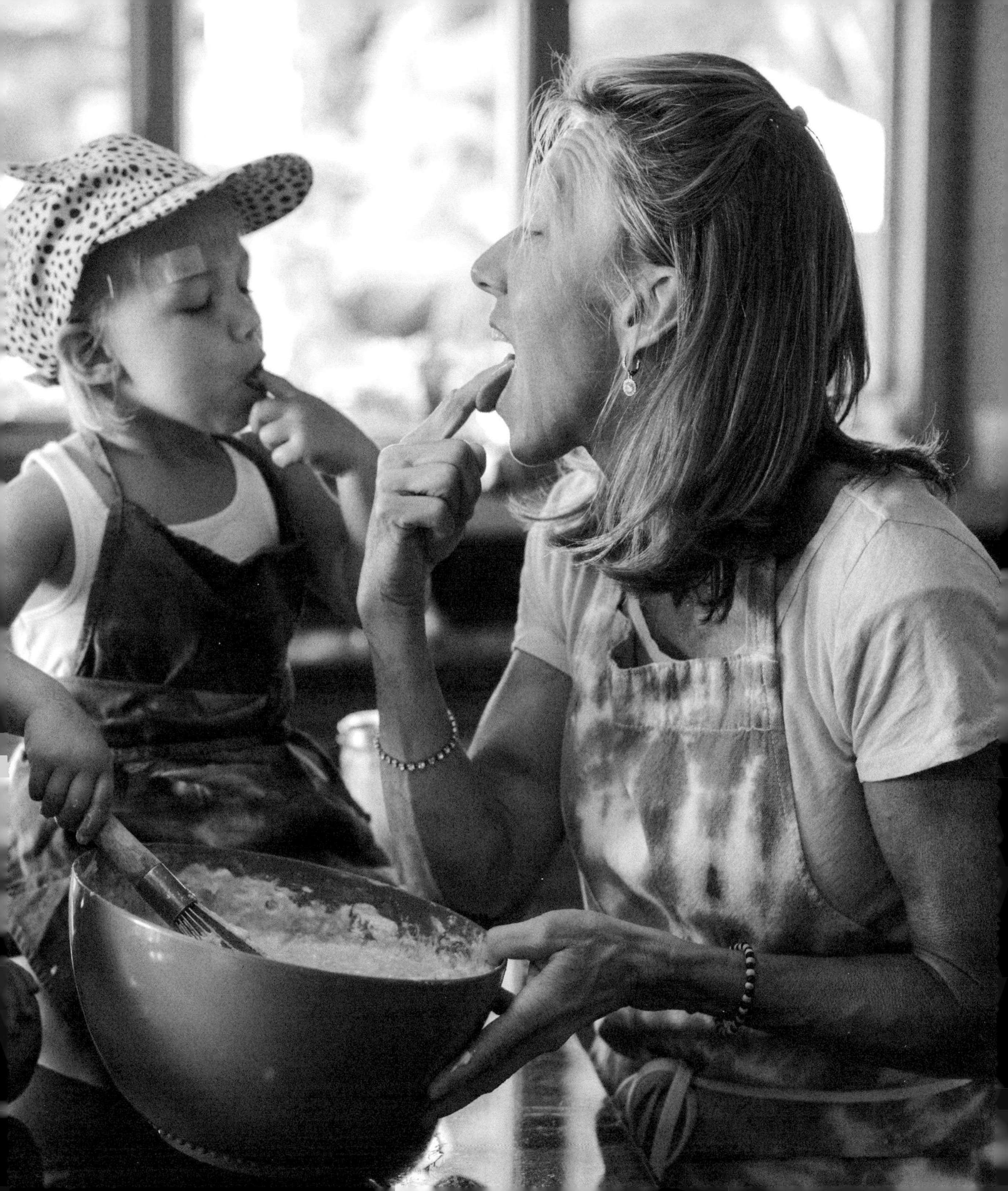

WHERE THERE IS LOVE THERE IS LIFE.

Mahatma Gandhi

Mealtimes

In New Testament times, the Saints gathered daily, breaking bread and eating meat with gladness and singleness of heart . . . and praising God (see Acts 2:46–47). Somehow the gathering with homemade bread strengthened souls. It was part of the worship of their lives, this coming to the table. Perhaps it was a symbolic reminder that the Lord meets us in our hunger. He fills us. *Daily bread* is a reminder of His consistency in our lives, of the importance of being filled.

There is something binding about breaking bread together, knowing everyone is welcome here. Grace at the table. It is the time that is familiar, this gathering around the table. It has been said, "Perhaps nothing in the life of a household is of more importance than the daily meals."

Every afternoon, when four o'clock rolls around, I ask the same question: *What's for dinner?* Most days I am tired of trying to think of what to cook for dinner. I spend so many of the minutes of my day standing at the counter in the kitchen, and sometimes I am exhausted at the thought of the grocery store, and the menu planning, and the getting everything in the oven on time. I am tired of the complaining over the meal I choose to make. I wonder over the *why* of this mealtime gathering, and then I remember.

It was toward evening, after the day was far spent, when *He* sat with them. He broke the bread and blessed it, and their eyes were opened, and they knew Him (see Luke 24:29–31). *I want my family to know Him.* If it will take place over broken bread, if they will be filled, if strength will come from those moments at the table, then it is worth every effort.

Mealtimes aren't always hard. Sometimes our best meals are hot dogs around the campfire; conversations are sweet in the outdoors when the sun is setting and summer surrounds. Then there are the comfort foods, the meals people ask for when they are sick or after surgery or when it has been the worst day. I know when they ask for that meal that something in their soul needs mending.

My girls love to try out new recipes, to fill the counter with the mess of creating, and we laugh and learn together. Sometimes we eat mac and cheese. Or breakfast foods. Or freezer meals. Looking back, I realize it wasn't what I made for dinner that was important. It isn't the filling of bellies but the filling of souls that should guide my planning. And broken bread from the grocery-store bakery will fill the belly just as well as homemade does. It is the conversation that takes place over the bread that becomes important now.

What if the conversation at each meal was filled with intention? A checking in. An assessing of the soul. What if there were questions that became a part of every meal: *What was the sweetest part of your day, and what was the lowest moment? What were the pits and the peaks?* If the evening meal was a place for the downloading of the heart, maybe the evening prayer would reflect the pleading for specific and individual needs.

On some days you will notice the one who is struggling. You will see it when they walk through the door, defeated. *You will know.* Perhaps you keep a special plate for days like these. When that one sits down for dinner in front of the special plate, when the family gathers in, you will shower the downtrodden one with words that lift: *This is what I love about you, this is what I know about you, and this is what the Lord knows about you.* The safest of places should be reserved for the lifting of hearts. Let your table become a place to strengthen, to lift, to succor. Perhaps that special plate comes out for moments of celebration, for times of honoring, for the important days. But let its greatest use be for lifting the one. Maybe every so often you will invite someone new to your table—a neighbor, a friend, a grandmother, a nephew. The table can become a sacred place to minister to any of the loved ones in your life.

There was one mealtime tradition my family brought home with us from Mexico. The sun hung gentle over the concrete courtyard of the tiny orphanage. It was the ending of the afternoon and the settling in for supper. We stood on the edges of the crowd as the children gathered in, lined up by age. Five lines across, five children in each line. All looked to the one who was in charge of preparing the evening meal. Together, they started speaking at once, their sweet Spanish voices filling up the courtyard. I do not speak Spanish, but I could tell something important was happening. "What is it?" I asked the man standing next to me. "What is it that they all know how to say together?"

"It is a scripture," he whispered back. "It is from the book of John." I wanted to know more about this scripture that was repeated every single day just before the prayer over the food. I carried my *sopes* filled with lettuce and chicken and guacamole to the table and sat by one of the older boys. My friend, who could speak the language, interpreted for me. "Please tell me about the scripture," I asked the boy, and I settled in for the learning. He pointed to a blackboard hanging on the back wall, to the words written there. On it was the scripture they would memorize all month long. It was what they would repeat before each meal until it became a part of them, until they were all filled.

I saw the Lord's consistency in their lives. He is the daily bread. I witnessed His children being filled.

Is there a place for scripture at your mealtimes?

Perhaps you struggle gathering all of the family together. This is especially true when the children are in their teenage years. Sundays are the best for family meals. It is the day that is mostly quiet from soccer and from school and from social events. Could this meal become the highlight of the week? Maybe you will set a beautiful table with your best china, linens, and fresh flowers in the vase that waits empty. *Maybe.* But if that overwhelms you, remember how one of the Lord's best

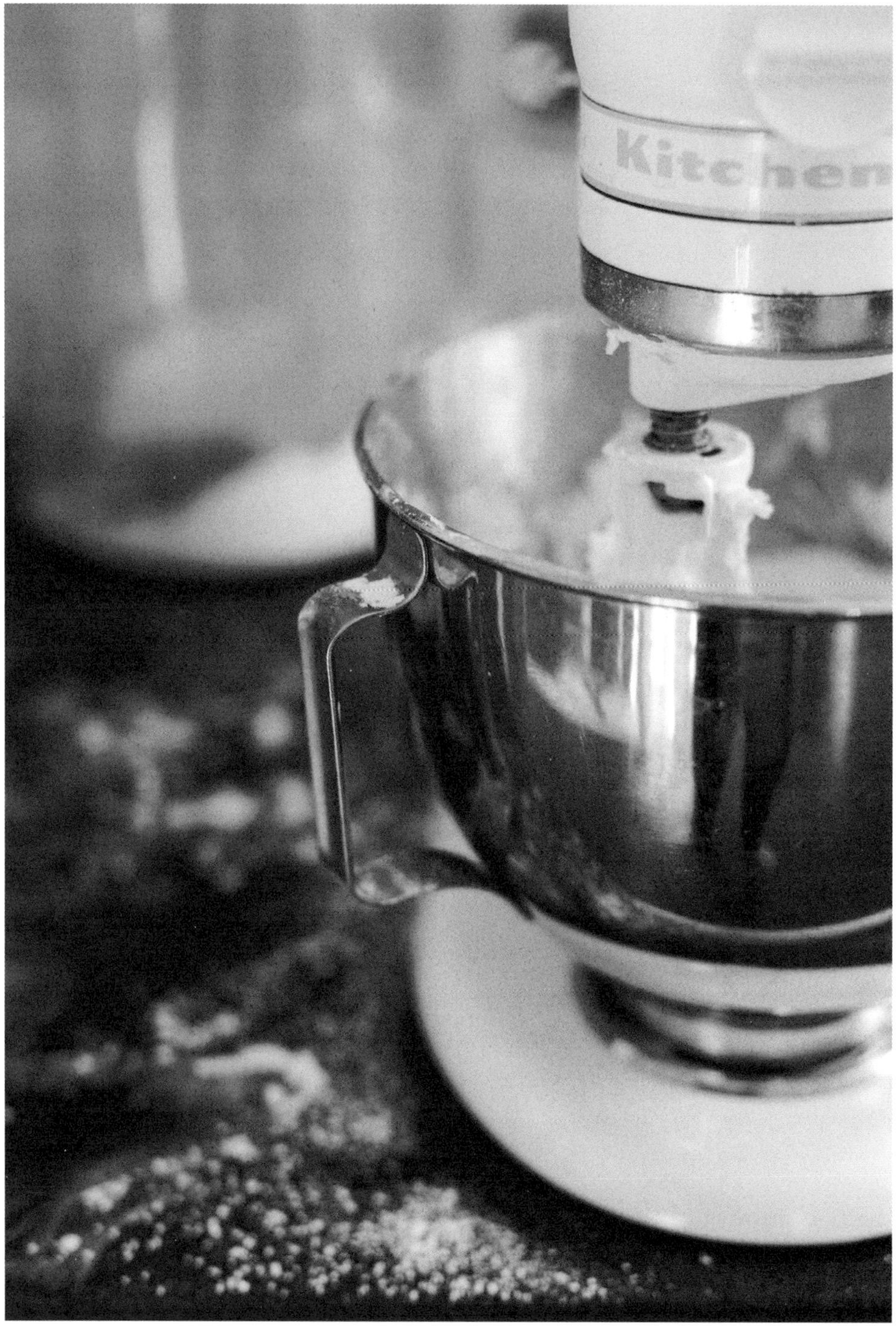
Kitchen

meals was in a wilderness place where everyone ate bread and fish while sitting on the grass. You will know what to do. Be intentional, but be you. Then miracles will come. Souls will be filled.

Gather daily. Break bread. Come to the table.

What will this look like for your family?

Take time to fill out your mealtime goals on the planning pages at the back of this book. They might look something like this:

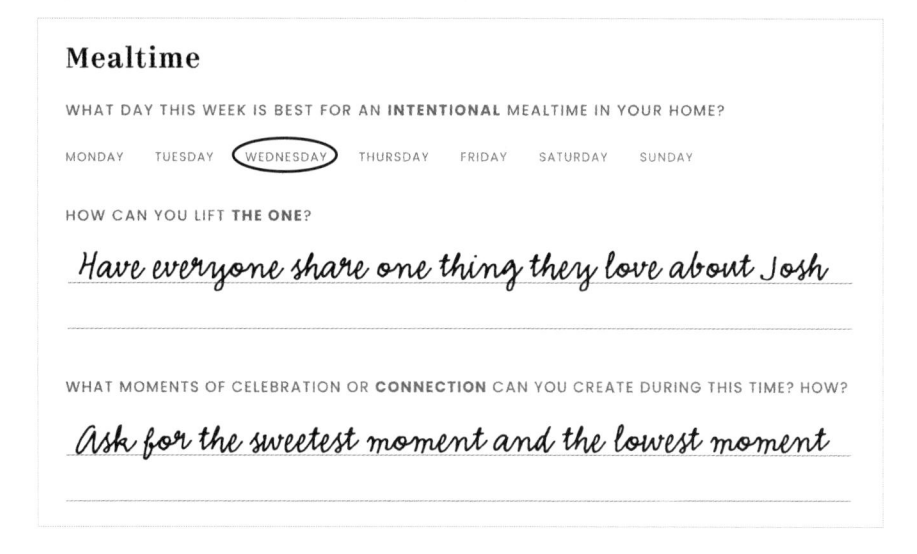

Mealtime

WHAT DAY THIS WEEK IS BEST FOR AN **INTENTIONAL** MEALTIME IN YOUR HOME?

MONDAY   TUESDAY   (WEDNESDAY)   THURSDAY   FRIDAY   SATURDAY   SUNDAY

HOW CAN YOU LIFT **THE ONE**?

Have everyone share one thing they love about Josh

WHAT MOMENTS OF CELEBRATION OR **CONNECTION** CAN YOU CREATE DURING THIS TIME? HOW?

Ask for the sweetest moment and the lowest moment

How will you make mealtimes an intentional part of your gathering home?

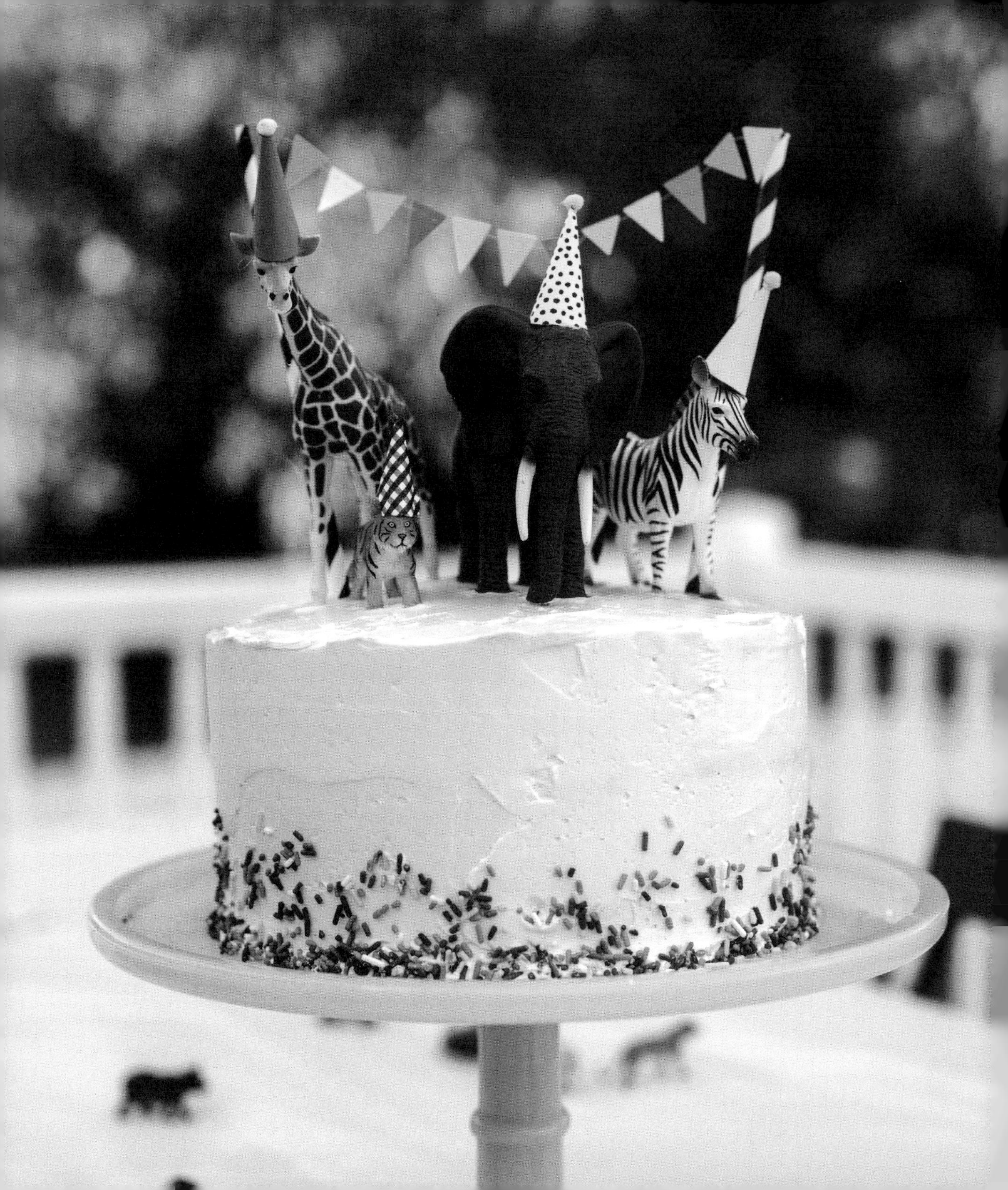

> FOR WHERE TWO OR THREE ARE GATHERED TOGETHER IN MY NAME,
> THERE AM I IN THE MIDST OF THEM.
>
> *Matthew 18:20*

Rites of Passage

There will be momentous occasions in life. One of the earliest is the first birthday celebration, the baby in the high chair with chocolate cake and frosting from the fingertips to the elbows, in the hair, the chocolate covering everything except those deep brown eyes. And then, it's every birthday after, when the family gathers and, for one day out of 365, *you* are the celebration of life.

It's turning eight and the looking for rainbows and the earth right after rain, the receiving of the unspeakable gift, and you are a covenant keeper now. Or eleven, and one weeknight is set aside as sacred, and you receive a recommend, and you are taught about temples and the ministering of angels.

It's waiting for *the call* to come and putting your life on hold in order to share the good news. It's finding a white gown. It's devoting your life to the cause of your country. It's heading off to college, and graduation, and the good you will add into the world.

These are the days to be remembered, the moments we hold onto: rites of passage. How you will capture each of them is up to you. But for one small moment in time, that one person will feel celebrated. Remembered. Important.

These are significant days for significant people.

These are days worth the creating and the gathering and the giving.

Celebrating doesn't look the same for everyone, and maybe you are overwhelmed with the images and thoughts of what things should look like. Put aside social pressures and just do exactly what calls to you. On most occasions you will create something simple and deliberate; at other times you may feel the call to create a visual celebration to be remembered. What matters most is simply that you honor the important occasions. These are the days that make up the living.

Plan the celebration.

Take time to make goals to commemorate rites of passage. We have included three sets of planning worksheets for your rites of passage at the end of this book (see page 225). If you need more, feel free to make copies.

How will you make rites of passage an intentional part of your gathering home?

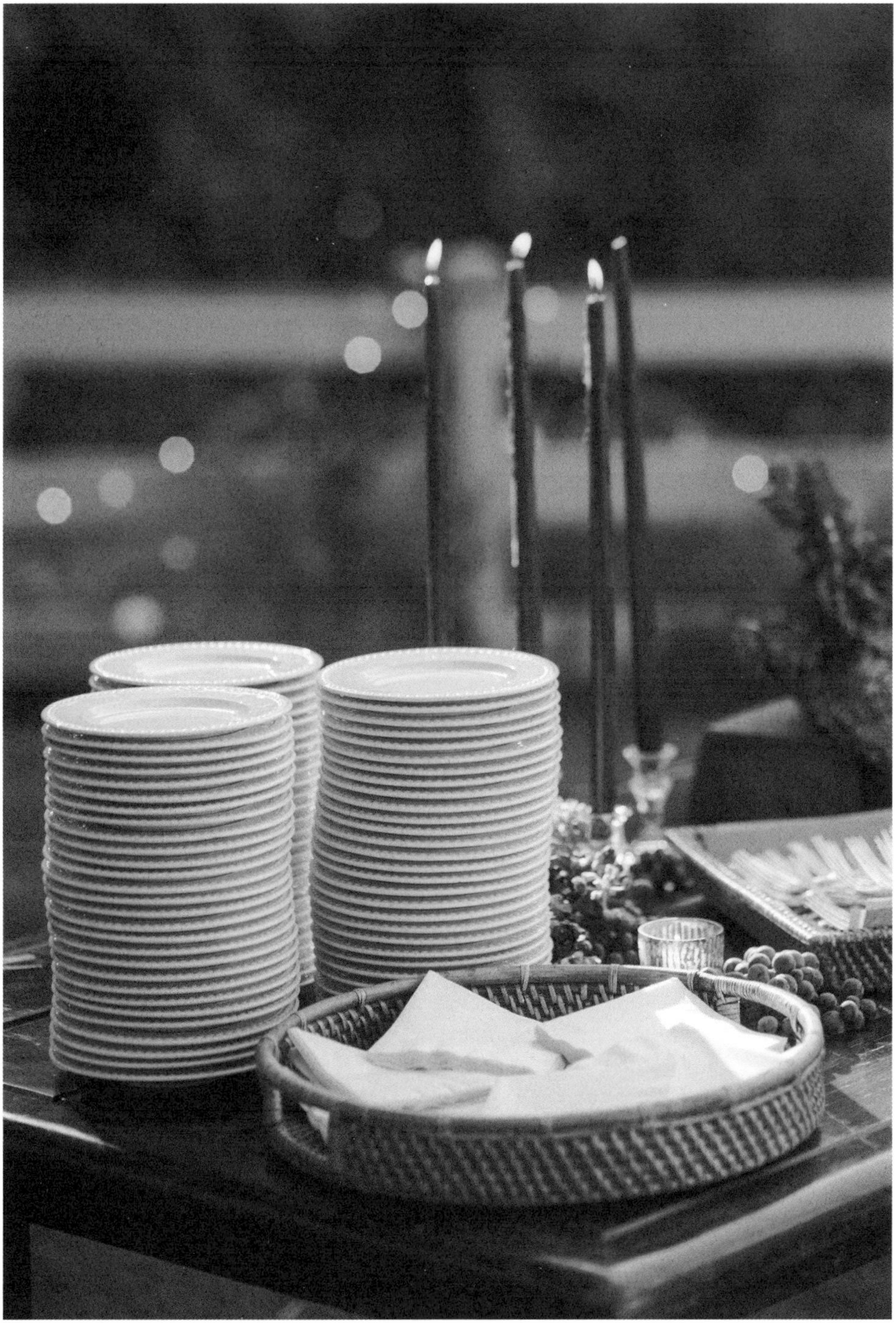

PART TWO

THE CELEBRATION OF SEASONS

*It is the letting go of the past and the welcoming of the future.
It is new intentions, a fresh start, beginning again. Days that are growing longer,
sparkling white snow, soft blue and midnight skies, gray clouds with silver linings.
It is warm woolen mittens and cocoa warming on the stove.*

IT IS JANUARY.

January

Gray clouds fill up heavy and roll across the sky. Snow falls on tree branches somewhere in the world. The beginning of the year is thick with gathering in. We seek shelter—if not from the weather, then from the world. January is beginning again, starting over. Perhaps you already have fond traditions, but if you need some more ideas, here are some thoughts for a January evening at home.

THE BEST DAYS DINNER

George Durrant once wrote a book with the title *My Best Day So Far*. In it, he wrote about how he learned to look back at his life and focus on the good things, changing his perspective. What would happen if we were to take some time in our own lives to look back at our best days? What if we devoted one specific day each year to do that?

January is a good time for looking back as well as forward. Perhaps you could choose one day at the beginning of January and start a new tradition: The Best Days Dinner.

The idea is to create an evening meant to help define perspective by pointing out the best things in our lives. Perhaps the whole evening could be based on everyone's best things. You could ask for everyone's favorite to cook for dinner. You might purchase special drinks to put by everyone's place setting instead of name cards, and each person could find their seat by looking for their favorite drink. Maybe it will just be a dessert night with an offering of everyone's favorite sweet treat in the center of the table. Your gathering could take place the first week of January.

Several days before the gathering, you might send an invitation to every guest or member of the family. Ask them to come prepared to answer two questions. First, *What is the best thing that happened to you last year?* Invite them to bring a picture to show, or a trophy, or a report card, or a dried rose, something to represent that day. Ask them to tell the others about that best day, the memory they don't want to forget. The second question is, *What do you think will be the best part of this upcoming year, and how are you preparing to make that happen?*

Let each person take a turn to share their answers while you are eating. You might consider purchasing a small family journal that you pull out every year on this night, a Best Days Journal that you can fill up with your family's very best days over the years. — INSPIRED BY KATIE

INDOOR GAME NIGHT

When we play together, we also laugh and learn together. Games allow us to connect across generations, cultures, classes, and interests. There is also something nostalgic about teaching our kids the games we grew up playing. Remember how being old enough to join in the adult games was almost like a rite of passage, making you feel special and grown up? Games force us out of our comfort zone and create moments that are memorable and bonding. Your game nights might be so much fun that you will decide to host one every month!

The number-one tip for game night is to choose a quick and easy dinner so you leave as much time as possible for the games. Maybe you will have pizza delivered, or you could consider just having hors d'oeuvres placed strategically throughout the game room. A specialty drink station would be fun for this event

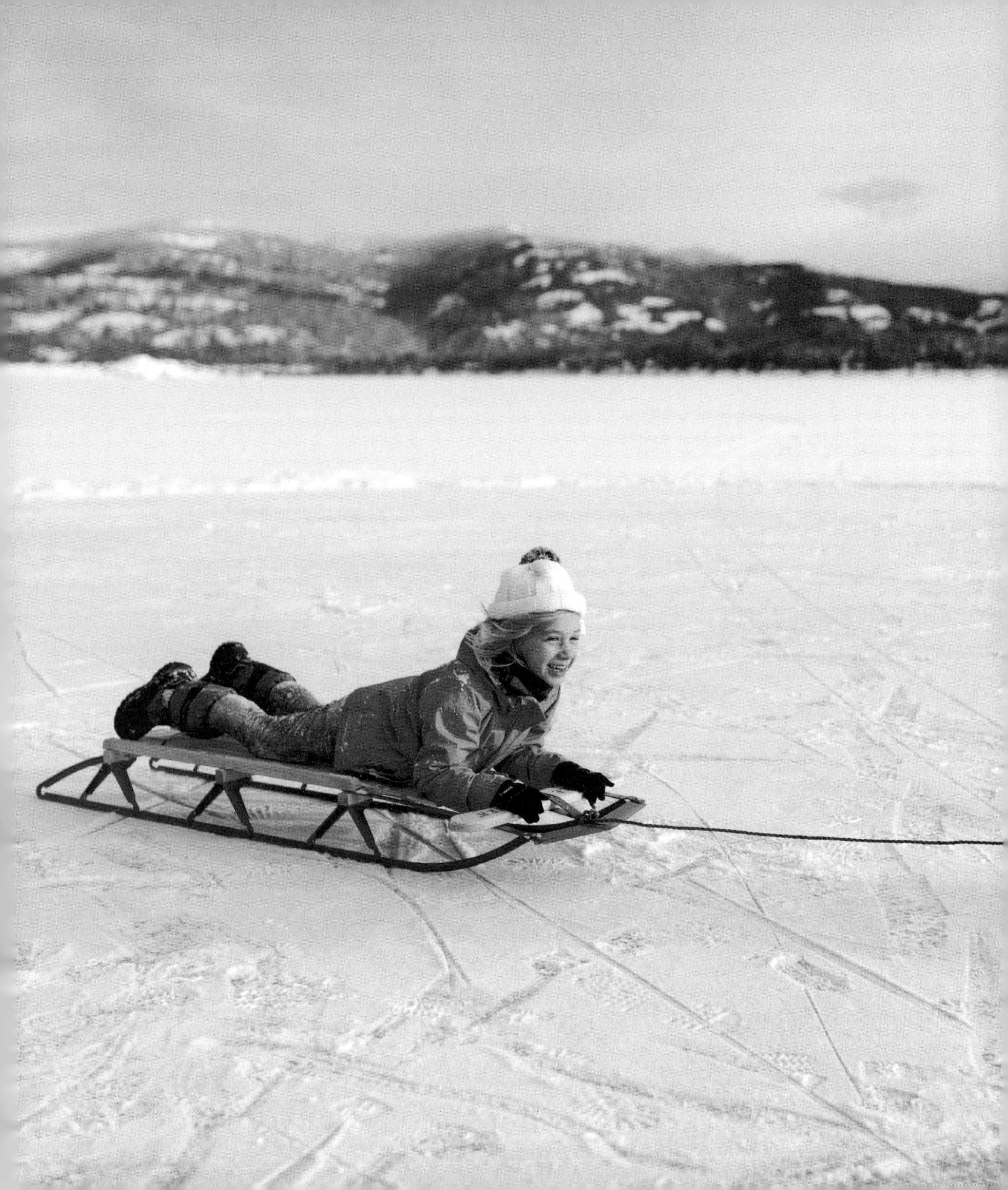

as well—perhaps an Italian soda bar or a tin barrel filled with all different kinds of soft drinks. Place treats in bowls on the tables. Pretzels, chips, popcorn, chocolate candies, or nuts would all work great!

If there are a lot of people coming, you might consider having a couple of board games set out along with a puzzle. If you have a smaller crowd, just choose three or four board games and switch things up after you finish each game. You can find all sorts of free games on the internet to play with a group, including spoons, Pictionary, and charades.

One of our favorite games is called the Flour Game. All you need is a cookie sheet, a bowl, a fresh bag of flour with enough flour to fill your bowl to the top, a penny, and a kitchen knife. Begin by putting the penny at the bottom of the bowl; then pour the flour all the way to the top of the bowl. You will need to pack it down as if you were building a sandcastle. When it is packed tight, turn the bowl upside down on the cookie sheet and lift the bowl off. You should have a mound of flour with a penny on the top. Each person takes a turn cutting away part of the flour until the penny falls. Whoever cuts the last slice of flour just before the penny falls has to retrieve the penny with their mouth, ending up with a face full of flour! Once the penny is retrieved, begin the game again.

A fun idea for game night would be to give prizes. You could even make a coveted trophy that is passed around year after year—something unique or funny that will add laughter to your evening of togetherness. — INSPIRED BY JESS

SEASONAL PLANNING PAGES CAN BE FOUND ON PAGE 233.

A GOOD LIFE IS A COLLECTION OF HAPPY MEMORIES.

Denis Waitley

*It is taking a deep breath and settling in next to the warmth of a fire.
It is handmade valentine cards, candlelit dinners, and chocolate strawberries.
It is remembering and cherishing one another. Pink candy hearts, deep red roses,
and white antique lace. It is love spilling over to family and neighbors.*

IT IS FEBRUARY.

February

February evenings are for pink and red construction paper and white doilies on valentine boxes. They are for picking out a box of cards from the grocery store and signing your name thirty-two times. February is an expression of love. Perhaps you will host a dinner with red roses in a vase, heart-shaped sugar cookies, and conversation hearts. If you are looking for something a little bit different, here are a few ideas.

※

CANDLEMAS

On the darkest of days, our hearts long for the brightest of lights. Perhaps your family would love to celebrate the "Feast of Lights," also known as Candlemas, a Christian holy day that commemorates the presentation of Jesus at the temple (see Luke 2:22–40). It is celebrated on February 2, which is halfway between the winter solstice and spring equinox.

Many families celebrate Candlemas by gathering as many candles as they can find and lighting them throughout their houses for the entire evening. On this night you might consider avoiding the use of electricity and performing every task by candlelight. A traditional Candlemas dinner consists of simple pancakes or crepes.

Consider adding strawberries, raspberries, whipping cream, and chocolate syrup to give the meal more of a Valentine's theme. It might be fun to eat dinner by candlelight and then read a story by candlelight before bed.

On Candlemas, with the house filled with the flickering lights of so many flames, some families teach about Jesus Christ being the light of the world. Perhaps before tucking everyone into bed and blowing the flame of each candle out, you will talk of ways you can reflect His light. — INSPIRED BY KATIE

DELIVERING FLOWERS

Several years ago, a good friend shared his experience of what was almost the worst Valentine's Day ever. He had experienced a bad breakup the night before and woke up on Valentine's Day feeling sad and discouraged. But then the Spirit whispered, *There are people sadder than you today. Who won't receive any flowers?* My friend acted on that prompting. For the remainder of Valentine's Day, he delivered flowers to those who were spending the day alone. He ended up at his grandmother's house at the end of the night with one last rose. "What are you doing here?" she asked. "Why aren't you out with your friends?" He explained what had happened and where he had been all day. "Your grandfather would be so proud that you remembered me," she said. Now delivering flowers is his Valentine's Day tradition. He does it every year.

Maybe you will consider delivering flowers, or chocolates, or homemade cards on Valentine's Day. You could stop by the homes of people in your neighborhood who might be spending the evening alone. It might become the best Valentine's Day you have ever had. — INSPIRED BY EMILY

VALENTINE'S WEEK

Perhaps Valentine's Day in your family isn't about elaborate gifts or grand gestures. Maybe you prefer handwritten notes and homemade valentines. One family we know spends the entire week before Valentine's Day celebrating. The parents take one child out at a time to a restaurant of the child's choice. It is a quick evening out with Mom and Dad, a night when the kids get one-on-one time. The dates are created to make sure each child spends the evening feeling important, answering personalized questions, being listened to and individually loved. The time involved is a sacrifice with reward. Perhaps that many nights going out to dinner won't work for your family. Consider shorter trips for dessert right after school or after dinner. Go for a sundae, or a special drink, or maybe even a slush. Where you go doesn't matter as much the individual attention. — INSPIRED BY JESS

SEASONAL PLANNING PAGES CAN BE FOUND ON PAGE 233.

HOME SHOULD BE AN ANCHOR, A PORT IN A STORM,
A REFUGE, A HAPPY PLACE IN WHICH TO DWELL,
A PLACE WHERE WE ARE LOVED AND WHERE WE CAN LOVE.

Marvin J. Ashton

*It is ivy on the trellis. The new green of tender grass.
It is the soft cream wool of newborn lambs.
It is the breath of life and growth and creation.
It is coming alive again.*

IT IS MARCH.

March

You may already be planning to dress in green and dye the scrambled eggs and pancakes for St. Patrick's Day. You will wish your loved ones luck and pinch those who forgot to wear the right color. When March comes in like a lamb, you won't forget the traditional celebrations. But perhaps you would like to experience a different gathering this March. Here are some ideas.

GENERAL CONFERENCE

This is the month you will want to prepare for general conference because the preparation will take place in the last week of March and the very first days that welcome April. (Additional suggestions for creating a memorable gathering for general conference can be found in the section for September.) We have included a special general conference template in the Planning Pages section so you will have room to capture everything you feel inspired to do. This gathering is unique in that the preparation is important to the success of the gathering itself. We invite you to make all of the preparations in the days leading up to general conference so that you can sit with your family and enjoy conference once it begins.

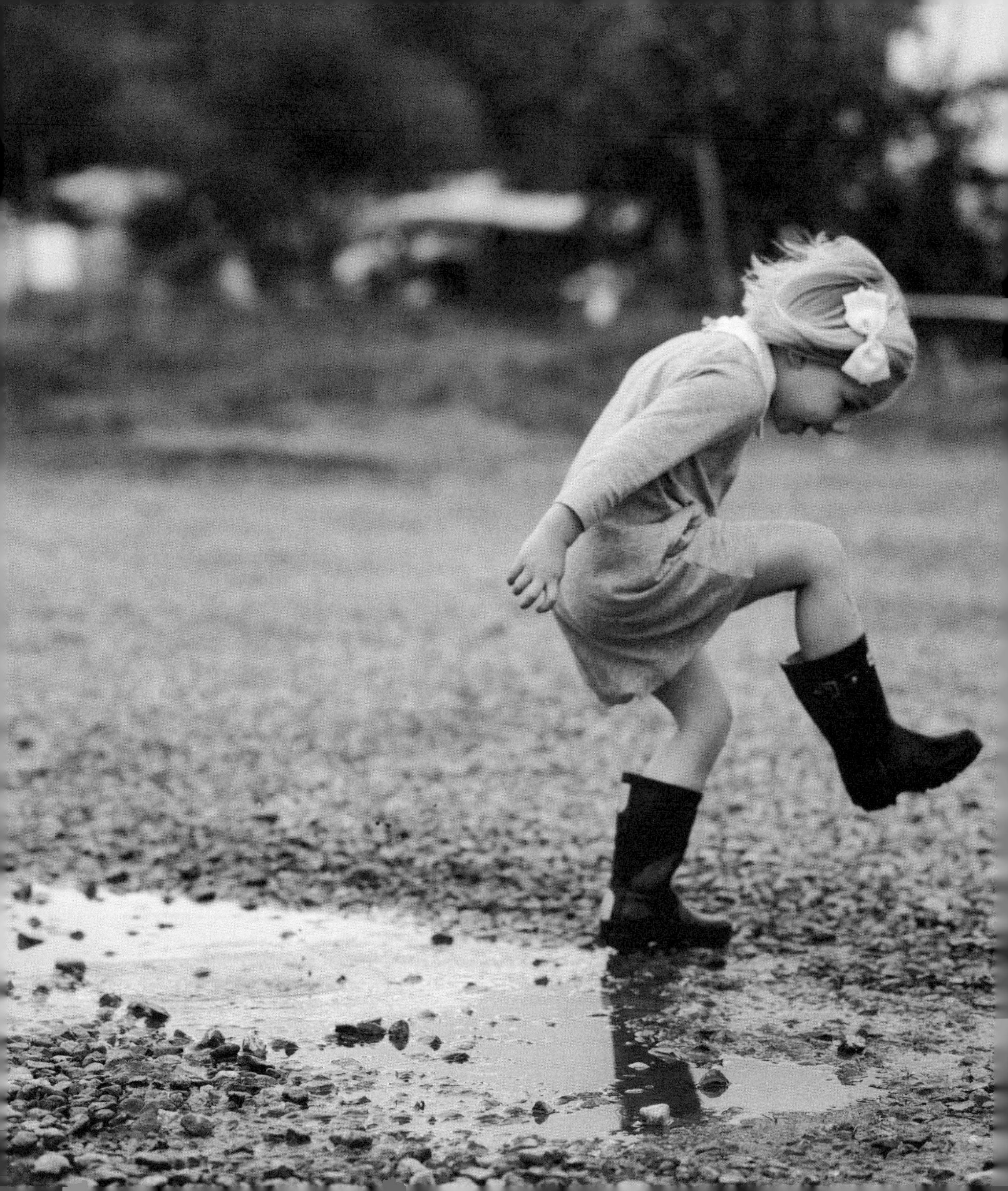

The general conference template includes three sections: preparing for learning, preparing for meals, and preparing for between sessions.

Preparing for Learning

How you will prepare depends on who you will be watching conference with! If you are watching with young children, you might think of things like conference bingo, coloring pages, or other helpful tips and tools that can be found in many places online. As your kids grow older, you might purchase a small journal for each one and invite them to write two or three personal needs in the front of their notebooks as a reminder to listen specifically for those things. Some families invite their kids to come up with one specific quote that stood out to them from the conference. You might print out those quotes and hang them somewhere special in your home to remember for the next six months.

Preparing for Meals

Take some time to prepare snacks and meals you wouldn't necessarily have time for on other days. Whipping up homemade cinnamon rolls or chocolate chip cookies in between sessions is always fun! You could also have an omelet bar, a taco bar, or Hawaiian haystacks. Let every person choose a favorite treat and leave all the goodies out to snack on over the course of the two days. Be creative and choose snacks and meals people will look forward to.

Preparing for Between Sessions

Conference weekend is such a great time for gathering. During the sessions, things will be quiet as people are listening. Between sessions is a perfect time to have some fun. What new recipes could you try? If the weather is good, perhaps you could plan a soccer game or other outdoor activity in between the two Saturday sessions. At night you might gather for dessert to talk about what you have learned. Maybe there will be special dinners for those attending the evening conference session.

There are so many places to fill with gathering during the conference weekend. It is the preparation in the week before that will create a spiritual weekend your family will remember. — INSPIRED BY KATIE

THE STRENGTH OF WOMEN PARTY

There is a remarkable strength that comes when women gather together. March is a month for celebrating the society of women—we celebrate the Relief Society's birthday this month. But what about a gathering to celebrate your own society of the women surrounding you?

Plan a special evening to gather the women who fill your memories and are woven into the fabric of your life. This should be a night of connection and strength, a time of inclusion. You may invite close friends from over the years, or women in your neighborhood, or all the women in your family. We know of a group of women who gather because they have all lost babies. Another family gathers all of the women age eight and older together once a year to talk about the remarkable women in their family history. Many women gather friends who have been influential in their lives for a special dinner to honor them. Consider inviting each guest to bring one of her favorite things and gift it to someone else who is attending the gathering, or have everyone bring a scripture that is meaningful to them written on a piece of paper and let guests choose one to take home with them.

You might consider a personal gift to honor each woman. One of our favorite traditions for this is a cake pull. Here's how it works: Prepare or purchase a beautiful cake. You will also need to purchase enough small bracelet charms for every woman attending the party. Tie each charm to the end of a beautiful piece of ribbon. Before you place the cake on the serving dish, put the charms in a circle in the middle, with all the ribbons coming out from the middle and over the edges of your dish. Place the cake right on top of the circle of charms. Before you serve the cake, ask all of the women to stand in a circle around the cake. Have each of them choose one of the pieces of ribbon and hold onto it. Express your love and admiration for each person in the circle and then invite all of the women to pull their charms from under the cake. Each woman's charm becomes your wish for her this upcoming year. — INSPIRED BY KATIE AND EMILY

SEASONAL PLANNING PAGES CAN BE FOUND ON PAGE 233.
GENERAL CONFERENCE PLANNING PAGES CAN BE FOUND ON PAGE 259.

CREATE OF YOUR HOMES SANCTUARIES OF HOLINESS AND STRENGTH.

Joseph B. Wirthlin

*It is the celebration of the Resurrection of Christ.
Creation coming to life where winter has been. It is deep purple hyacinths,
pink tulips, and bright yellow daffodils. It is wicker baskets, gathering eggs, and
Cadbury chocolates. It is the whisper of hope and promise and life.*

IT IS APRIL.

April

This is the season of Eastertide, with new baby chicks and soft bunnies and chocolate. April also whispers of white Easter lilies and resurrection hope. It is a season of sweetness and peace. Easter will sometimes fall in April, and sometimes in March. We invite you to arrange your planning of general conference and Easter according to which one comes first.

NEIGHBORHOOD EASTER EGG HUNT

Occasionally, you might want to invite your entire neighborhood or your extended family to participate in a gathering. An Easter egg hunt can be an easy event for a large gathering.

Consider hosting an Easter egg hunt on a Friday evening or Saturday morning before Easter. Choose a park near your house or hold the event in a cul-de-sac in your own neighborhood (making sure you get permission from all the homeowners). Send out invites a week before. On the invite, ask every family to bring one dozen candy-filled eggs for every member of their family who is participating. (So, if they have four kids participating, they will bring forty-eight eggs.) You might leave a huge wicker basket on your porch and ask people to drop the eggs off at your home the day before the hunt. Invite children to bring their own Easter baskets for gathering. Arrange for some teenagers in your neighborhood to come help hide the eggs two hours before the hunt.

Consider dividing the space into three areas, each for a different age group. One yard or space would be for toddlers. Another space would be for five- to nine-year-olds, and the third space would be larger (perhaps two household yards) and would be for children ten and older. When the families come, gather everyone together and explain the rules: Each child should take home only twelve eggs, and everyone should stay in the area designated for their age bracket. If they find more than their share of eggs, they will need to share with someone who didn't find as many.

Neighborhood gatherings are unique in that they have the power to strengthen both individual families and also communities. The best moment of this event is when everyone first gathers, before the hunt begins—families huddled together waiting for the instructions, children with anticipation on their faces, and adults building friendship with one another. There is a spirit of love, and unity, and coming together. That is the blessing of gathering. — INSPIRED BY EMILY, KATIE, AND JESS

SERBIAN EASTER SUPPER

There are many wonderful ways to gather for an Easter supper. Traditionally, a formal dinner is held on Easter Sunday after church. Perhaps this meal is the one time each year when you bring out the china.

Traditions

You may have your own special traditions about gathering the family for Easter. Perhaps you eat ham and scalloped potatoes; maybe you stay dressed up in your Sunday best. You might read an Easter poem before you begin, or celebrate with a picnic, or serve brunch. We have discovered a wonderful tradition from Serbia that we love incorporating into our celebration. In Serbia, during the years when the government outlawed discussing religion, it was a tradition for many families to gather together behind closed doors to decorate eggs on the night before Easter. They used skins from yellow onions, which would die the eggs a deep red. It was the grandmother's role to teach the family about Jesus Christ on that one night of the year. The families would display those red eggs on their fireplace mantels all year long as a witness of their belief and for good luck.

In honor of this Serbian tradition, perhaps the culminating event of your Easter dinner could be to invite the oldest woman at the table to bear her testimony of Jesus Christ. Maybe it will become the sweetest part of your Easter meal, something your children will never forget.

Preparation

If you decide to try the Serbian tradition of red-dyed eggs, you will want to start your preparation several days in advance. You will need the skins of twelve yellow onions to dye your eggs. Place the skins in a large pot with plenty of water. Bring the water to a boil, boiling for fifteen minutes to let the skins dye the water. Leave the skins in the water and let the water cool to room temperature. Once the water is completely cool, place brown eggs into the pot with the skins. If you want one egg for every person coming to your Easter dinner, you should cook four more eggs than you need in case one or two crack. Hard boil the eggs in the onion-skin water, then leave them in the water overnight. (You will not be eating these eggs, so this is fine.) The next morning, take the eggs out and let them dry. Once they are completely dry, rub each egg down with a napkin and olive oil. You might want to purchase egg holders to display the eggs.

If you set your table on Saturday night, it will help make the dinner something to look forward to all day long. You might place a huge bouquet of white Easter lilies in the middle of the table. Set out each of your place settings, and then, once all is ready, set out one red egg next to each place setting so that every person who attends will have a reminder of your Easter dinner: a beautiful red egg to keep somewhere special until Easter comes again. — INSPIRED BY EMILY

SEASONAL PLANNING PAGES CAN BE FOUND ON PAGE 233.

'TWAS EASTER-SUNDAY. THE FULL-BLOSSOMED TREES
FILLED ALL THE AIR WITH FRAGRANCE AND WITH JOY. . . .
WE BOTH OF US FELL DOWN UPON OUR KNEES
UNDER THE ORANGE-BOUGHS, AND PRAYED TOGETHER.
I NEVER HAD BEEN HAPPY TILL THAT MOMENT.

Henry Wadsworth Longfellow

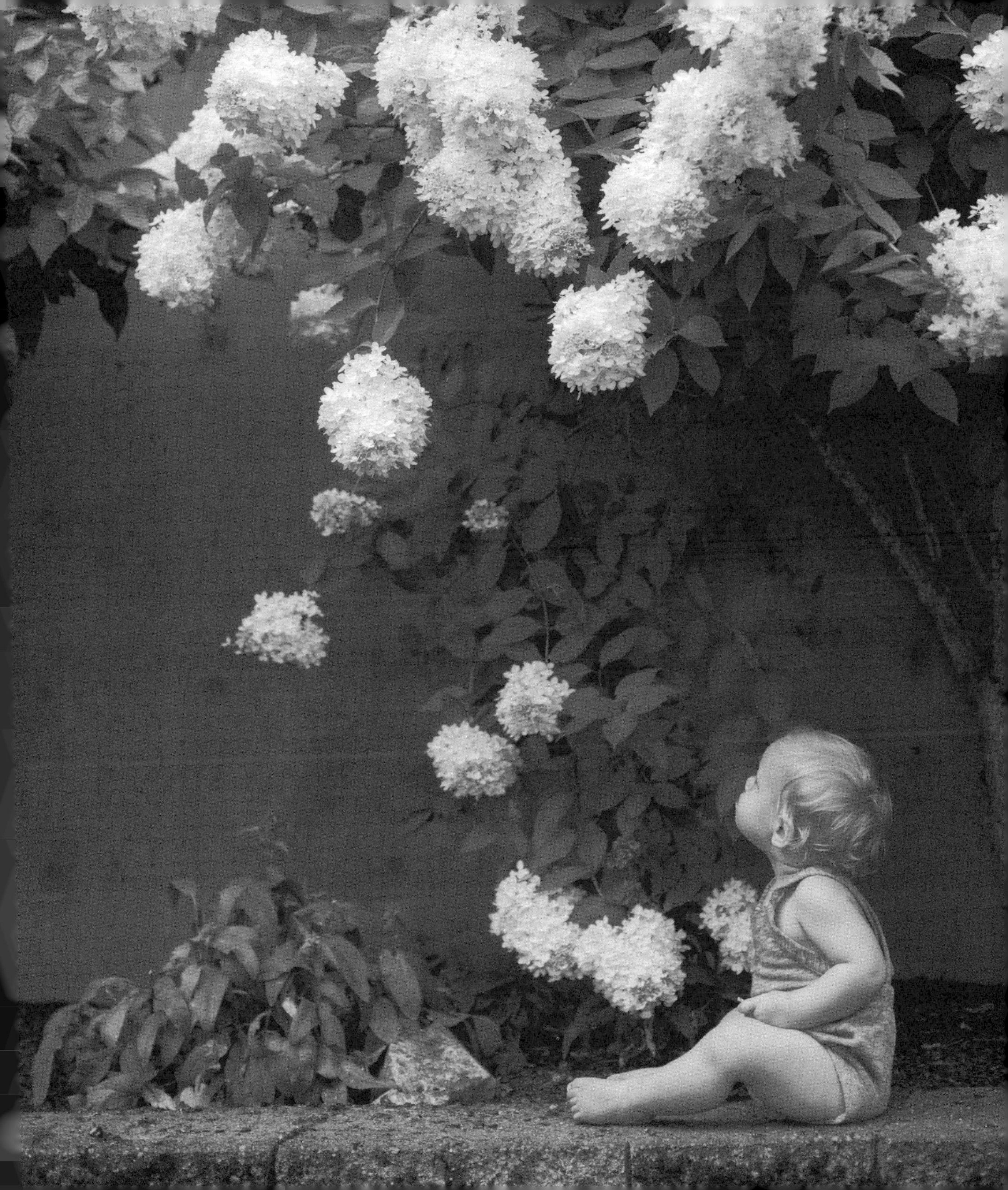

It is visiting graves and remembering stories of the past.
It is a graduation from early bedtimes and strict schedules.
It is planting red petunias, yellow summer squash, and green peppers.
It is the chirping of birds in the backyard again.

IT IS MAY.

May

The last days of the school year are filled with end-of-year parties, and yearbooks, and carnivals. The cleaning of desks and of lockers and the putting away of backpacks open up the hours of the day for so many other things. As the days lengthen, we start spending more evenings outside. Neighbors gather on porches, we go for evening walks, the smells from summer barbecues fill the air. These are the days for making memories. We have a few memory makers we think you might love.

PLANTING PARTY

As the weather starts to warm up, anything that takes place outside the home is a welcome adventure. That is one reason we love the idea of a planting party so much! First, you need to decide what you want to plant and where. Maybe you have a garden out back. Perhaps you will plant flowers in pots to give as Mother's Day gifts or to place around the outside spaces of your home. Perhaps you will fill your front yard with petunias. You decide!

Your guest list may depend on what you are planting. If you are creating potted planters, you might decide to invite your mom and sisters or a group of friends from your neighborhood. Have everyone bring their own pot and enough flowers to share with the group. Each person can bring their own shovel to make preparation easier. When you are finished, everyone takes their own pots home. If you are planting a garden or flowers in the yard, you might let the kids in your family each take responsibility for readying the yard, choosing what to plant, and digging the holes. If you don't have kids at home, perhaps your next-door neighbors would enjoy having a planting party with you.

As you prepare for your gathering, remember to have plenty of water, sunscreen, and garden gloves on hand. You might consider preparing a picnic lunch with sandwiches and chips. Perhaps you will set out some fruit or simply have popsicles on hand. Lemonade and cookies on a side table in the yard could be really fun too! Enjoy the afternoon celebrating the idea of new life and the beginning of summer days ahead. — INSPIRED BY KATIE

MOTHER'S DAY

Mother's Day is a day for feeling gratitude for and honoring the important women in your life. Whether those women are mothers, aunts, or mentors, make sure you take the time to express your appreciation for their influence in your life. You might consider planning a brunch the Saturday before Mother's Day just for mothers and daughters. It could become a memorable occasion to celebrate the women of your family or neighborhood.

Our favorite gifts we have received on Mother's Day over the years are the homemade cards our children have made. Perhaps those are your favorite as well. Maybe you keep them in a drawer next to your bed and read them from year to year. There are few things that make us smile the way those cards from elementary-age children can.

As you prepare for Mother's Day, consider setting aside an evening for making homemade cards. Purchase specialty paper with fun colors and patterns. Spend time cutting out hearts or flowers and gluing them onto your cards. Make sure you take time to write a meaningful message inside each one. Lists can be powerful—try writing a list of things you love about your mom. Wouldn't it be fun to give her a keepsake box to keep all of her cards in over the years? What if you read the cards from past years out loud as a tradition on Mother's Day? This is just one simple way to pay tribute to the influential women in your life. — INSPIRED BY EMILY, KATIE, AND JESS

REMEMBERING THE PAST

For many families, Memorial Day starts with a restaurant breakfast. The extended family meets at a restaurant in the early morning and enjoys pancakes, bacon, eggs, and orange juice. Once breakfast is over, everyone piles into cars and follows each other from one cemetery to the next. Perhaps some sit in the grass under the shade of the trees nearby and listen to stories of family members they have never met: the brother who died when he was so young, the mother who fought valiantly for her health, a grandfather who fought in World War II and overcame hardship. This day is a day for celebrating the heroes in our families.

Memorial Day is a time for remembering. It doesn't matter if you are close to the places where your family members are buried or if you are far away. We can all gather around for breakfast and stories of strength and courage, love and faith, loyalty and sacrifice. These are the stories that bind us together, stories that give confidence and build character. There is something empowering about knowing where you came from. That knowledge becomes the material from which we build our own dreams. — INSPIRED BY EMILY

SEASONAL PLANNING PAGES CAN BE FOUND ON PAGE 233.

I SUSTAIN MYSELF WITH THE LOVE OF FAMILY.

Maya Angelou

*It is long days and fair weather.
Summer solstice, night games, and swing sets.
It is lying on your back in the cool grass and watching the clouds float by
and midnight stargazing in the backyard. It is bare feet in riverbeds.*

IT IS JUNE.

June

June is the month when you feel like setting the calendar aside. It's a time for slowing down and settling in. Firepit nights in the backyard, at the park, or up in the mountains with roasted marshmallows and Hershey bars. Husking corn on the cob and chatting on the back porch. The gatherings that fill this month beg to be held outdoors. Here are a couple to consider.

FATHER'S DAY

It is not often that we take time to express gratitude to our fathers. This is a day for doing just that! Most days, Dad's is probably the alarm that goes off first, and perhaps he is the first to leave. He rarely has time for breakfast and never has breakfast in bed, so maybe his day could begin with that. If he is a lover of cereal, maybe you could go all out with favorites, even if he has more than one bowl on the tray. Maybe there will be a mountain man breakfast with bacon, sausage, hash browns, and eggs. You will know what is best.

Maybe the evening meal is a casual event. Perhaps you will gather for a family barbecue with watermelon, sweet corn on the cob, hamburgers, hot dogs, and fun drinks. Once dinner is cleaned up, you could serve root-beer floats. You might sit out on the back deck under the umbrellas and talk for hours.

This celebration is not so much about what you do; what is important is who you are with. It is about quality time, and laughter, and relaxing together, and celebrating Dad. — INSPIRED BY JESS

SUMMER SOLSTICE

Did you know June 21 is the longest day of the year? A favorite tradition in our neighborhood is to stay outdoors that day until the sun goes down. Our whole neighborhood takes part in planning this event. The summer solstice party is simple, but so much fun. We send out invitations a week in advance. A big backyard, a cul-de-sac, or a park work really well for this gathering. Tell the families you are inviting to come after dinner and bring a package of popsicles to share with the group. Make sure you have enough freezer space for that many popsicles! If not, people could bring cookies or brownies or another simple treat. Put the desserts aside for safekeeping as people show up.

Night games are the agenda for the entire evening: kick the can, kickball, hide-and-seek, sardines, whatever outside games you can think of. The children and adults all play. If it's been a long time since you have participated in night games, look some up on the internet, or ask your kids! Twilight, the magic hour when all the world is tinted yellow, will last its longest on this night. When dusk finally begins to set in, after the sun sinks below the horizon, pull out the treats and let everyone sit around and enjoy each other's company.

One year our neighbor invited a musician to play music in the backyard. All the neighbors brought blankets and sat on the grass. We spent time relaxing and listening before we started the night games. It was magical.

These moments when you gather the neighborhood together, whether close-knit or spread apart, can be powerful for building relationships in your community. Consider pulling together an event like this once or twice a year. It will cost you nothing besides a bag of popsicles, but the memories and friendships created will be priceless. — INSPIRED BY EMILY

SEASONAL PLANNING PAGES CAN BE FOUND ON PAGE 233.

WE WERE TOGETHER,—
ALL ELSE HAS LONG BEEN FORGOTTEN.

Walt Whitman

*It is the crimson, navy, and crisp white of freedom waving in the summer breeze.
Watermelon. Fireworks. Hot dogs.
It is parades, and sparklers, and neighborhood breakfasts.
Car windows rolled down and children running through the sprinklers.*

IT IS JULY.

July

This is the month of pool parties, and summer picnics, and evening barbecues. Everyone comes out of their homes, and the neighborhood streets fill with people walking and talking, and friendships are renewed. It is a time for some of our very favorite summer gatherings.

FOURTH OF JULY BREAKFAST

Every Fourth of July at 8:00 a.m., you will find our family standing in front of our neighbor's flagpole with the rest of our neighborhood. The Boy Scouts raise the flag, and we all crowd around—all of us—from newborns to ninety-year-olds. We repeat the Pledge of Allegiance and sing "The Star-Spangled Banner." During the prayer on the food, we are reminded of our great nation and the freedoms we hold dear. Then we head for the pancake breakfast and impromptu parade, and we can't help but stop and look around at family members and neighbors gathered together. It's a moment for hearts to swell, overflowing with gratitude. It happens just the same way every year.

Perhaps you too will host a Fourth of July breakfast. This would work for a group of neighbors or a large extended family. Don't be overwhelmed by the magnitude of this idea—this gathering is easier than you think! You will want to find a cul-de-sac, or maybe consider using your church parking lot for this gathering. Your event could run from 8:00 a.m. to 9:30 a.m. It is a quick, fun, and easy way to celebrate the Fourth of July!

Preparation

For this event, you may want to ask a few other families to help you host. A couple of these host families will be in charge of the pancakes, syrup and butter, and paperware for the entire event. Two other families could host the parade and be in charge of crepe paper, balloons, and tape.

Send out invitations to all the families in your neighborhood. This could easily be a potluck breakfast, so on the invitation you might make the following assignments: families with last names starting with A–F bring a fruit bowl, families with last names starting with G–N bring a gallon of juice, and families with last names starting with O–Z bring muffins or donuts. Also invite everyone to bring a blanket or camp chairs to sit on. That way every family can set up their own eating area and take it home with them when they leave. Finally, make sure the kids know to bring a bike or scooter for the parade.

We do not include an event timeline for any of the other gatherings in this book, but we thought that understanding the particulars of this gathering would make it easier to execute, since so many people are involved. Feel free to adjust the following times for the needs of your guests.

7:00 a.m.: Setup begins. Put tents or canopies over the griddles. Set up banquet tables to collect the fruit, juice, and muffins, as well as the plates, pancakes, syrup, and butter. The parade decoration station can also be set up in the early-morning hours; one table holds all the balloons, crepe paper, and tape. Set up this station apart from the breakfast area in a driveway or other large space that provides room for everyone to decorate their "vehicles" for the parade.

7:30 a.m.: Start cooking pancakes; keep them warm on the griddle until breakfast begins.

8:00 a.m.: Greet people as they begin to arrive.

8:10 a.m.: Meet at the flagpole for the flag raising, Pledge of Allegiance, song, and prayer.

8:20 a.m.: Begin serving breakfast. As children finish eating, they can move over to the decoration station to dress up their bikes and scooters for the parade.

9:00 a.m.: Begin the parade.

9:30 a.m.: End the event by thanking everyone for coming and beginning cleanup.

Parade Tips

Put a car at the beginning and a car at the end of the parade to keep everyone safe. Tell the kids to stay in between the two cars for safety. The children could go around the block one time and then roll by all of the guests still sitting in the chairs.

You will be surprised by how easy this gathering is to set up and how quickly it takes place. We think it will become one of your favorite neighborhood events.
— INSPIRED BY EMILY AND KATIE

PIONEER WALK

Pioneers are an important part of our cultural heritage. On July 24, 1847, the first group of Latter-day Saints arrived in the Salt Lake Valley after being forced to leave their homes in Nauvoo. Today, July 24 is a day devoted to celebrating the pioneers and their sacrifices. Even if Pioneer Day is not a recognized holiday where you live, you can still set time aside to enjoy remembering the stories and sacrifices of pioneers. Sometime this month you might consider organizing a pioneer walk in remembrance of those early Saints who walked across the plains. Perhaps you will walk five miles or ten miles. We know of one family who walked seventeen miles, and some families have walked twenty-four miles in remembrance.

Here is what your gathering might look like. Choose a pioneer you want to celebrate, and plan how far and what route you will walk in remembrance of that person. You might find stories of your own ancestors that list how many miles they walked in one day. Consider pausing two or three times on your walk for breaks to sit and discuss the pioneer you are walking for. An easy walk for most families is five or six miles. That length allows you to walk two miles and then stop to talk about the pioneer you have chosen to remember that year. Focus on what you admire about that person, what you learn from their story, and how you can become more like them. These walks have the potential to create some great memories.

If you want, invite other families to join you. Make sure to bring enough water and snacks. For long walks, you will want to ask someone to follow in a rescue vehicle just in case someone needs a little rest. You don't need to travel all the way to Wyoming to experience a pioneer trek. You can re-create one in your own neighborhood. There's something about the stories and the walking that will bring a pioneer experience to life. — INSPIRED BY EMILY

SEASONAL PLANNING PAGES CAN BE FOUND ON PAGE 233.

> CELEBRATE . . . EACH DAY TOGETHER AS A
> TREASURED GIFT FROM HEAVEN.
>
> *Russell M. Nelson*

*It is the rediscovering of routine.
School shopping and new teachers and old friends.
It is yellow no. 2 pencils with black lead tips, brown paper sack lunches,
and standing in line for the bus. It is school days and summer nights.*

IT IS AUGUST.

August

August is the balance of holding onto summer and the looking forward to the new season ahead. It is new goals, and new direction, and new purpose. It's the last of the summer nights, and diving into the school year. This month we are giving you ideas for both.

ICE CREAM NIGHTS

Making homemade ice cream is the perfect way to celebrate late-summer Sunday nights. Maybe you will gather outdoors for a family dinner, where you can hear the ice-cream makers churning as you eat. If you have a large family, you will want to make two or three batches of ice cream. You can easily discover recipes you will love on the internet, but here's one family favorite we want to share with you. It is a beloved recipe that came by mistake. Someone didn't follow the instructions. They were supposed to be making chocolate ice cream, but they didn't realize they had to let the cream come to room temperature before they poured the melted semi-sweet chocolate into the liquid. Instead of blending smoothly into the cream, the chocolate hit the cool liquid and hardened immediately, splitting into tiny pieces. The resulting mixture became a family favorite: gourmet chocolate chip ice cream.

On those August nights, after the motors on the ice cream machines stop, you will gather. You might consider serving your ice cream in large paper cups rather than bowls, because homemade ice cream is soft like a shake. Make sure there is enough ice cream for seconds, and even thirds. Perhaps you will sit in the shade on the back porch and listen to the summertime sounds as they fade away, and you will laugh and soak in the last of those summer memories. — INSPIRED BY EMILY

BACK-TO-SCHOOL DINNER

Preparation for a back-to-school dinner begins by choosing a theme for the school year. Here are some ideas to get your imagination going. Maybe it will be "You Are Light," and the decorations would become encouragement for being a light wherever you go. Another idea could be "Life Is Like Riding a Bicycle," and you might teach the importance of balance and moving forward. Another idea is "The Future Is as Bright as Your Faith," and you might teach your children about faith over fear. Every year the theme can be something new.

If you choose to do this gathering, let the Spirit guide your efforts! Listen to what God is whispering to you at the start of each school year. Think of each of your children, their struggles and their hopes, and choose a theme that will lift and strengthen your kids as they go out into their world every morning. We often go all-out for neighborhood or church gatherings, but sometimes it is worth creating a spectacular evening meant specifically for your children. The gathering doesn't have to be expensive, but it should be fun and memorable.

Consider giving an invitation and a gift to each child for the school year ahead. You could, for instance, give everyone in the family a new pair of socks—crazy socks that go clear up to the knees—that somehow correspond with the theme of the evening. Maybe the socks will have rulers or rainbow stripes or palm trees on them. Let the gift become your symbol of family unity, a memory from your night of building strength before facing the new year ahead.

To help them remember the theme, you may want to print out a related quote for them to put in their room, as well as a family scripture or a general conference talk that teaches about the theme.

For the meal, envision a casual dinner with fun decorations—bright colors, specialty paper plates, and a centerpiece that reflects the theme. Don't feel like your night has to be serious or fancy. One of our favorite yearly themes included a pink VW bus, baseball hats, chicken tacos, bottled pop, and chocolate ice cream bars. The theme was "The World's Your Oyster, Dude!" We used the article "Faces and Attitudes," by Thomas S. Monson from the September 1977 *New Era*, and the following quote illustrated our theme for that year:

> *The happy life is not ushered in at any age to the sound of drums and trumpets. It grows upon us year by year, little by little, until at last we realize that we have it. It is achieved in individuals, not by flights to the moon or Mars, but by a body of work done so well that we can lift our heads with assurance and look the world in the eye. Of this be sure: You do not find the happy life—you make it.*

This gathering is a way to welcome in the school year, the return of routine, in a new and relevant way. It is a perfectly intentional gathering, meant for the ones who matter most. — INSPIRED BY KATIE

SEASONAL PLANNING PAGES CAN BE FOUND ON PAGE 233.

MAKE NO SMALL PLANS. THEY HAVE NO MAGIC TO STIR MEN'S SOULS.

Spencer W. Kimball

It is a worn Levi jacket. It is sitting in the stands of a football game and raking fall leaves into huge piles in the yard. It is farmer stands with yellow spaghetti squash and ripe red tomatoes. It is abundance—having more than you need and sharing the harvest. It is the storing up for the winter ahead.

IT IS SEPTEMBER.

September

September is when evenings become cool again. There are sweatshirts and blankets and layers, and everything is cozy now. National Quiet Day in some locales signals the end of summer spontaneity and the beginning of fall serenity. It is reading books on the sofa and long evenings at home.

DAY OF ABUNDANCE

For many years, our stake celebrated a Day of Abundance. One weekend night in September, we would set up tables in the grass behind the church building for people to bring the excess from their summer gardens and their homes. We would pile the tables high with zucchini, butternut squash, tomatoes, peaches, cantaloupe, carrots, and potatoes. In one corner of the parking lot there was a large truck for people to donate old clothing, shoes, coats, and winter gear. In the center of the large field, there were hot dogs grilling, bags of chips of every variety, and ice-cold lemonade. Blankets were spread out all over the grassy hill. People would come and stay. They talked with neighbors and ate hot dogs on the lawn, and our community was strengthened by the giving.

Hands down, the best part of the event were the rows and rows of tables. At the end of each table were stacks of brown paper bags people could use to gather up the produce at the end of the evening to take home. The tables started empty, and they ended empty. People brought of their abundance and left filled.

This gathering symbolizes the scripture that reads, "Now at this time your abundance may be a supply for their want, that their abundance also may be a supply for your want. . . . He that had gathered much had nothing over; and he that had gathered little had no lack. But thanks be to God, which put the same earnest care into the heart . . . for you" (2 Corinthians 8:14–16).

This month, find a way to gather your people and share your abundance, whatever it may be. — INSPIRED BY EMILY

GENERAL CONFERENCE

General conference comes twice a year. Just like March, September is when you will want to begin preparing for general conference, since the conference takes place in some of the first days that welcome October. You can refer back to the March section for more general conference ideas, but we also want to give you a new set of ideas for the fall conference. We have included a special worksheet for general conference in the Planning Pages section, so you will have room to capture everything you feel inspired to do. Preparation is key to the success of this gathering. We invite you to make all the preparations in the days leading up to general conference so that you can sit with your family and enjoy conference once it begins.

The general conference worksheet has three sections: preparing for learning, preparing for meals, and preparing for between sessions.

Preparing for Learning

As you begin preparing for conference this month, think carefully about who you should invite. Maybe you will welcome someone into your home to learn with your family for one of the sessions of this conference. You might consider giving inexpensive gifts that make it easier to engage in the learning process, such as new journals and pens or even watercolor notebooks, paint, and paintbrushes to add some creativity to note-taking. Some families purchase special conference jammies

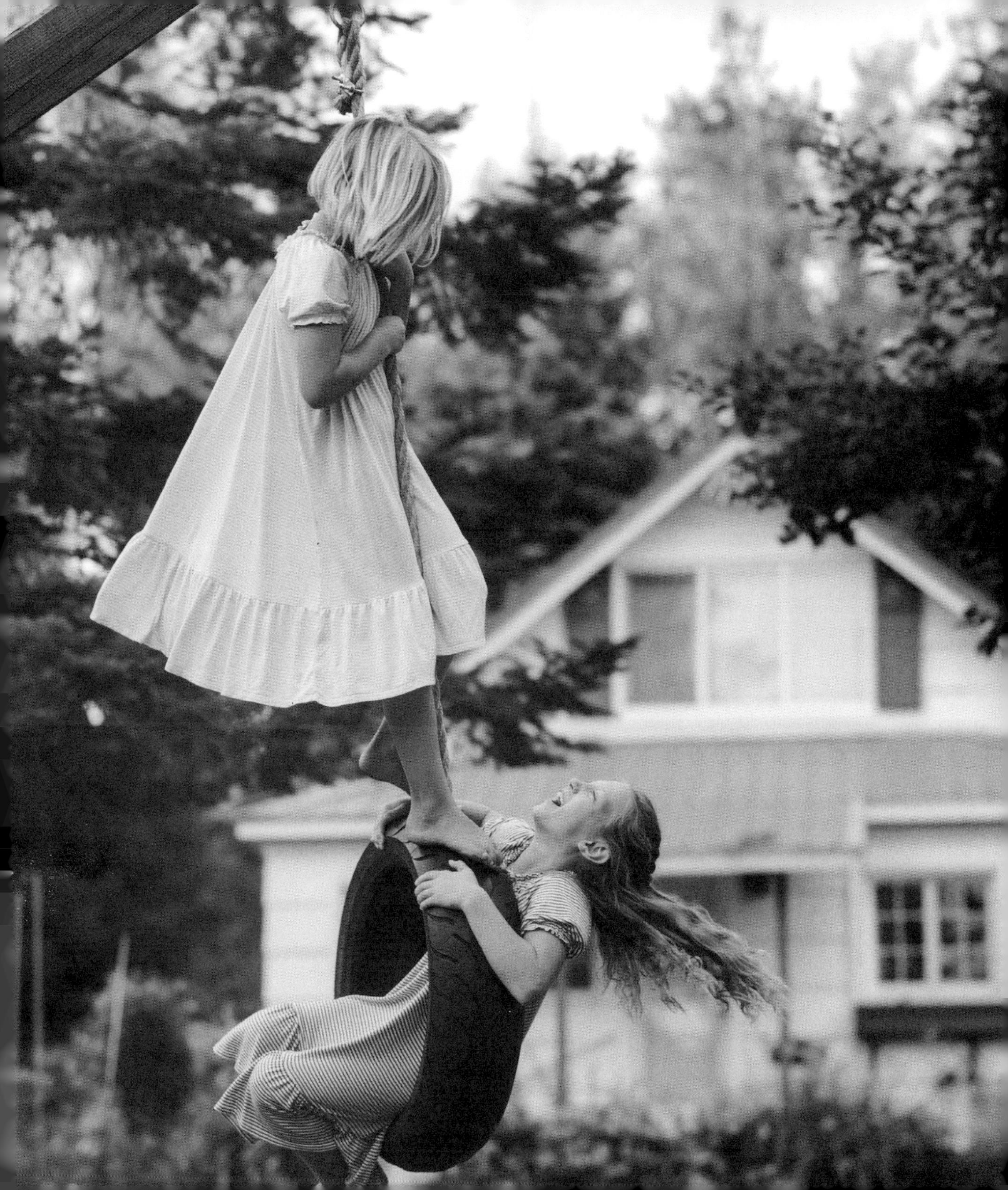

to remind everyone that the purpose of the day is to gather around the television and be still as they listen to the words of the prophet and the apostles and other Church leaders. Find creative ways to make general conference weekend something your family anticipates as one of their fondest gatherings.

Preparing for Meals

One ward we know hosts a general conference breakfast on the Saturday morning before conference begins. It is a continental breakfast with muffins, donuts, and all kinds of juices. Fifteen minutes before conference begins, everyone returns to their individual homes to watch the first session. A special breakfast might be something you want to do with your family, the neighbors on your street, or the people you minister to. Sharing a meal is a great idea for starting the weekend off in a special way. And it doesn't have to be a breakfast. You could organize lunch or even dinner at the end of all five sessions and invite everyone to share their takeaways from general conference.

Preparing for Between Sessions

Perhaps you will spend some time planning for the gatherings that will take place between sessions. Be prayerful as you consider how you will give love to those who you will be gathering with. Love can be expressed through the giving of time, the slowing down, the pausing to be with your loved ones. Take a walk together. Read through each other's notes. Spend some quiet time together on a blanket in the sun. Let the Spirit have a voice in deciding what will strengthen your family in between sessions. Blessings will come. — INSPIRED BY EMILY

SEASONAL PLANNING PAGES CAN BE FOUND ON PAGE 233.
GENERAL CONFERENCE PLANNING PAGES CAN BE FOUND ON PAGE 259.

THIS IS THE POWER OF GATHERING: IT INSPIRES US, DELIGHTFULLY, TO BE MORE HOPEFUL, MORE JOYFUL, MORE THOUGHTFUL: IN A WORD, MORE ALIVE.

Alice Waters

*It is caramel apples and warm cider.
The brilliant colors of fall hanging gently from the trees.
It is families gathering to hear familiar voices from the Conference Center.
It is carved pumpkins, bags filled with treats, and costume parades at school.*

IT IS OCTOBER.

October

Fall comes crisp on the air when October begins. You feel the hint of it and pull out the wool sweaters from the top of your closets. It is a season of warm soups and homemade bread, earlier bedtimes and cozying in. If you are looking for ways to gather and celebrate all of the goodness of fall, here are some ideas.

CARAMEL APPLE NIGHT

Caramel apples are the best fall treat, especially when they are homemade.

Maybe you and your loved ones will sit around the table and unwrap hundreds of Kraft caramels. Those clear wrappers will litter the table as you pile up the cubes in the pan. You will discover that the best caramel takes time. While someone stirs the caramels melting in the pan, the others can put wooden popsicle sticks into the waiting apples. Some like Red Delicious, others Granny Smith, but the sweetest apples are those whose skins hint of red and yellow at the same time.

When the caramels are all melted, after the mixture bubbles high, roll the apples in the pan until they are fully coated and then place them on wax paper on a cookie sheet to cool. It usually takes a whole evening to make caramel apples, everyone squished around the table unwrapping, stirring, and dipping. Those evenings around the table might become some of your favorite nights. — INSPIRED BY KATIE

DONUT DITCHING

What is it about fall and donuts? There is nothing like a hot donut right out of the fryer and drizzled with sugar glaze. One family we know goes donut ditching every year. They order twelve boxes of donuts and choose twelve families in their neighborhood to drop them off to. Stomachs fill with butterflies on those late nights when they drop the donuts off on another's porch, hit the doorbell, and run. Everyone dashes back into the car. Tires may squeal as it races down the street. *Who knew Dad could drive that crazy, right?* If you decide to do this activity, maybe the kids could be in charge of making cards to deliver with the donuts: "We donut know what we would do without you." Consider delivering to people in your neighborhood who are feeling spread thin, or who are lonely, or who could just use some extra love. This is a great way to teach your kids that service can be fun, a simple way of sharing some fall love. — INSPIRED BY JESS

HALLOWEEN CHILI NIGHT

I wonder who started the family tradition of making homemade chili on Halloween night. The best chili recipes are simple and never come from a recipe card. Here is one of our favorites: Start with a pound of bacon cut into one-inch squares. Then fry up some hamburger. Maybe you add black beans, fresh salsa, or V8 juice. Add a can of diced tomatoes, and don't forget to throw some spices in.

If word gets around about chili on Halloween night, you might need to cook the chili all day long in two huge pots on the stove. People will show up at all hours of the night because no one wants to miss out on a bowl of homemade chili. For us, Halloween is getting up and down every time the doorbell rings and sitting at the kitchen counter to talk with everyone who stops by. Chili has a way of bringing people in from the front porch, friends who will linger, who want to come and stay. We don't know why, but chili always suggests a gathering.

Sometimes what makes a holiday special is what sets it apart. Don't be afraid to come up with your own recipes, celebrations, and traditions for Halloween. Pass them down to your children. Bring people in. Leave your mark on the gatherings that make up your home. — INSPIRED BY EMILY

SEASONAL PLANNING PAGES CAN BE FOUND ON PAGE 233.

EVERY DAY IN YOUR LIFE IS A SPECIAL OCCASION.

Thomas S. Monson

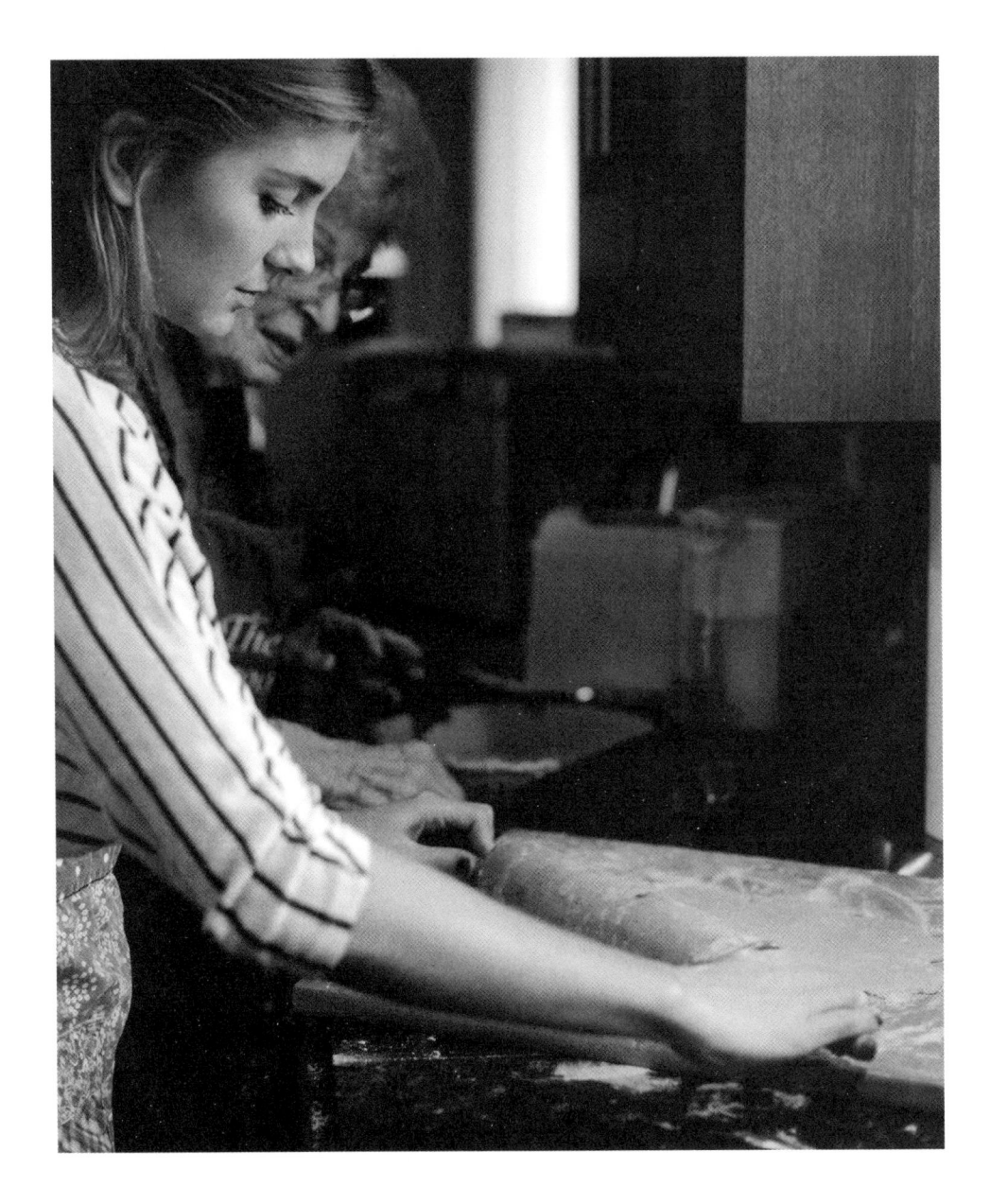

*It is family coming home again.
It is homemade rolls, stuffing, and mashed potatoes. Candlelight and the best plates and cornucopias. It is gathering recipes and sharing pie.
It is everyone around the table expressing what they are grateful for.*

IT IS NOVEMBER.

November

November whispers family. It is the month for gathering home. For our family, it is hanging a poster up on the pantry door, and people writing what they are thankful for every time they pass by it. It is the giving of thanks, hearts filled with gratitude, and remembering to appreciate our abundance. Besides Thanksgiving dinner itself, here are some of the other gatherings we love to host in November.

THANKSGIVING ACTIVITIES

We know many of you probably already have favorite family recipes, craft ideas for the kids, and treasured activities, like a good game of flag football, but here are a few ideas for other Thanksgiving traditions. Consider a family service project after dinner and before dessert on Thanksgiving Day. Let the assignment pass to a different member of the family each year; the person in charge will coordinate everything that is needed for people to participate on that day. Another favorite tradition that we all have in our homes is keeping a gratitude journal. One person is the scribe, and before the Thanksgiving meal is served, that person writes down the one thing each person is most grateful for from the past year. If you decide to keep a gratitude journal, store it with your Thanksgiving decorations so that it will be easily accessible from year to year. — INSPIRED BY EMILY, KATIE, AND JESS

PIE NIGHT

Before Grandma died, she took each of her granddaughters aside, one at a time, and taught them the art of making a homemade pie—how to get the crust just right, the secret to the filling. She was an expert at making pies; apple pie was her best. Grandma was genuinely famous for her pies, and she wanted to share her gift with her granddaughters. There is something special about handing down the important things. And she handed down more than just a pie; she passed down a piece of her heart that would reveal itself again every time Thanksgiving came around. Those pie-making dates are what her grandgirls remember most about her. She is gone now, but every year they call each other to see how each other's pies turned out. Each pie reminds them of her and all that she taught them, and pie still has a way of connecting them to each other.

There is something about a pie that gathers family. For each of us, a favorite Thanksgiving tradition centers on pie making. One family has five grown daughters. At the beginning of November, they each begin searching for pie recipes.

Each girl chooses her own. On the Wednesday before Thanksgiving, they go shopping together for all the things they will need for Thanksgiving dinner, including pie-making supplies. The cooking for Thanksgiving dinner begins in the morning. Every girl takes a different part. Once the dinner is totally prepared, they clean off all the counters, and the kitchen is quickly transformed into a bakery. Everyone has her own space for creating the pie she will share for Thanksgiving dinner that year.

Every year this family has five different pies for dessert. The pies take up the whole middle of the table as if they were the centerpiece. It is a favorite Thanksgiving Day tradition.

The kitchen is one of our favorite spots for gathering. If you haven't tried something like pie night, you should. Sweet conversations happen over kitchen counters. Memories are made. — INSPIRED BY EMILY, KATIE, AND JESS

STIR-UP SUNDAY

This gathering is an Anglican tradition that has roots in Great Britain. It takes place on the last Sunday before Advent begins and gets its name from a phrase in the Book of Common Prayer: "Stir up, we beseech thee, O Lord, the wills of thy faithful people." Over the years, that phrase has become associated with stirring up the Christmas pudding. In Britain, Christmas pudding is a type of boiled pudding made with dried fruit, but any pudding will work for your own Stir-Up Sunday.

According to tradition, the family gathers together after dinner to stir the pudding. The whole family makes the recipe together, and then every family member takes a turn stirring. When it is your turn to stir the pudding, you get to make a wish for the upcoming year. The pudding is supposed to be stirred from east to west to honor the journey of the three wise men.

Some families add a single almond to the mixture during the stirring process. Whoever gets the almond in their bowl when the pudding is served receives good luck for the year ahead.

It is the name of this holiday that catches our attention—*stir up*. We love the idea of a stirring up that takes place just before December comes. We believe that a season of gratitude prepares the heart for a season of giving. Maybe a Sunday in between Thanksgiving and the celebration of Christ's birth can be a time to prepare our hearts for the upcoming season. A stirring up.

Perhaps, as you eat your pudding that night, you could make a list of everything you and your loved ones hope will happen during the Christmas season. What traditions will you celebrate? How will you serve others? What will your gatherings look like? Let your hearts be stirred up with the anticipation of good things to come. — INSPIRED BY EMILY, KATIE, AND JESS

SEASONAL PLANNING PAGES CAN BE FOUND ON PAGE 233.

GRATITUDE IS SAID TO BE THE MEMORY OF THE HEART.

Joseph F. Smith

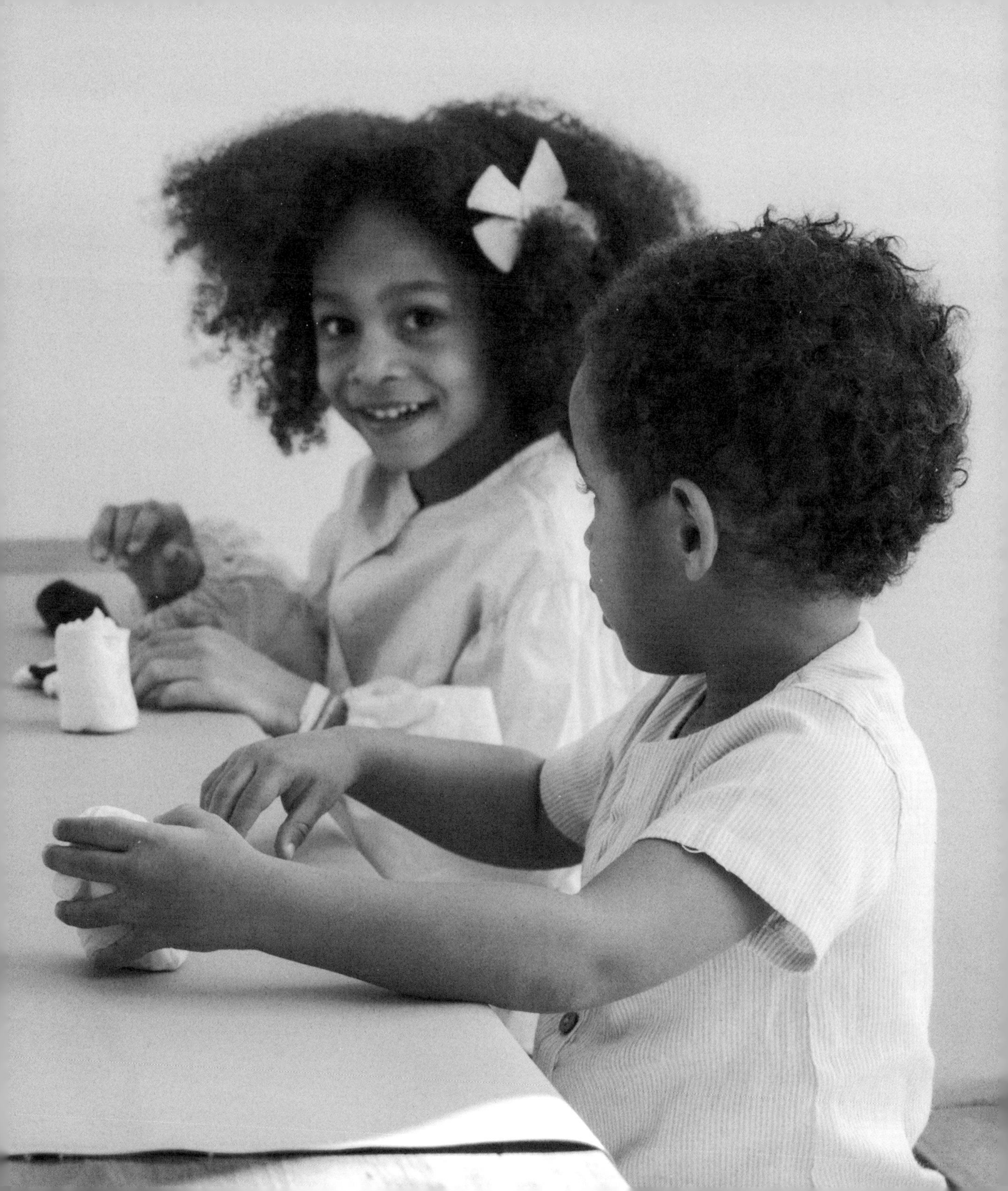

It is stockings hung by the fire, twinkling lights, and carols.
It is decorating the tree. It is a spiral-cut ham, matching pajamas, and gifts wrapped up in red and green. It is baby Jesus in a manger, shepherds watching their sheep, and wise men who followed a star. It is the joy of believing.

IT IS DECEMBER.

December

December is a month of tradition, of gathering, of family. Of all the months, this one holds a special place in our hearts. There are books filled to the brim with Christmas ideas and traditions and recipes. You certainly already have traditions that are dear to you, but in case you are looking for something a little different, we are sharing a few lesser-known holiday gathering ideas. Perhaps one of them will spark an idea for a gathering in your home.

ST. LUCIA DAY

We love the idea of going back to your roots as you plan your Christmas traditions. Katie's family loves to celebrate St. Lucia Day because her ancestors are from Scandinavia, where the holiday originates. This holiday is celebrated on December 13, and it honors St. Lucy, who wore a candlelit wreath on top of her head to light the way as she carried food to Christians hiding in catacombs. For many, this event signals the arrival of Christmastide. For some, the holiday is symbolic of Jesus Christ, born on Christmas Day, who brought light into a world of darkness.

In many Scandinavian homes, the oldest daughter dresses in a long white gown with a red ribbon tied around her waist. She wears a green wreath with lighted candles on her head and travels from room to room bringing sweet bread, cookies, and other desserts to all the guests who are there. St. Lucia Day is symbolic of so many of the things we want our children to learn: the importance of being bringers of light, of being brave and strong, and of being willing to carry light and love to others.

What is a holiday tradition that represents your ancestors? We invite you to spend some time discovering what celebrating such a tradition might look like in your home. — INSPIRED BY KATIE

SPONTANEOUS CAROLING

This gathering is so much fun! Start out with one or two other families and begin visiting the homes in your neighborhood. After you carol at a home, invite the family there to put on their warm clothes and come join you. By the end, you will have a whole group singing together from house to house. It would be fun to have a bunch of cookies ready for everyone to celebrate together at the end of the evening. — INSPIRED BY KATIE

LITTLE CHRISTMAS EVE

On the night before Christmas Eve, you might consider organizing a simple service project for your family. Go to the grocery store and purchase everything that you would need for a beautiful Christmas Eve dinner. You might choose a turkey or a ham, rolls, potatoes, and ingredients for your favorite side dishes, along with a poinsettia and a beautiful dessert. Drop off the food in a beautiful box on the front porch of a family in need. Once everything is set out just right, ring the doorbell and sneak away. It is a meaningful way to let the gift giving begin. — INSPIRED BY JESS

LUMINARY SHOW

A simple way to create the feeling of gathering in a neighborhood without having to schedule an event is to invite everyone to participate in a neighborhood luminary show. We have experienced this in several different neighborhoods on Christmas Eve. Early in the week, drop off a white paper sack filled with sand and

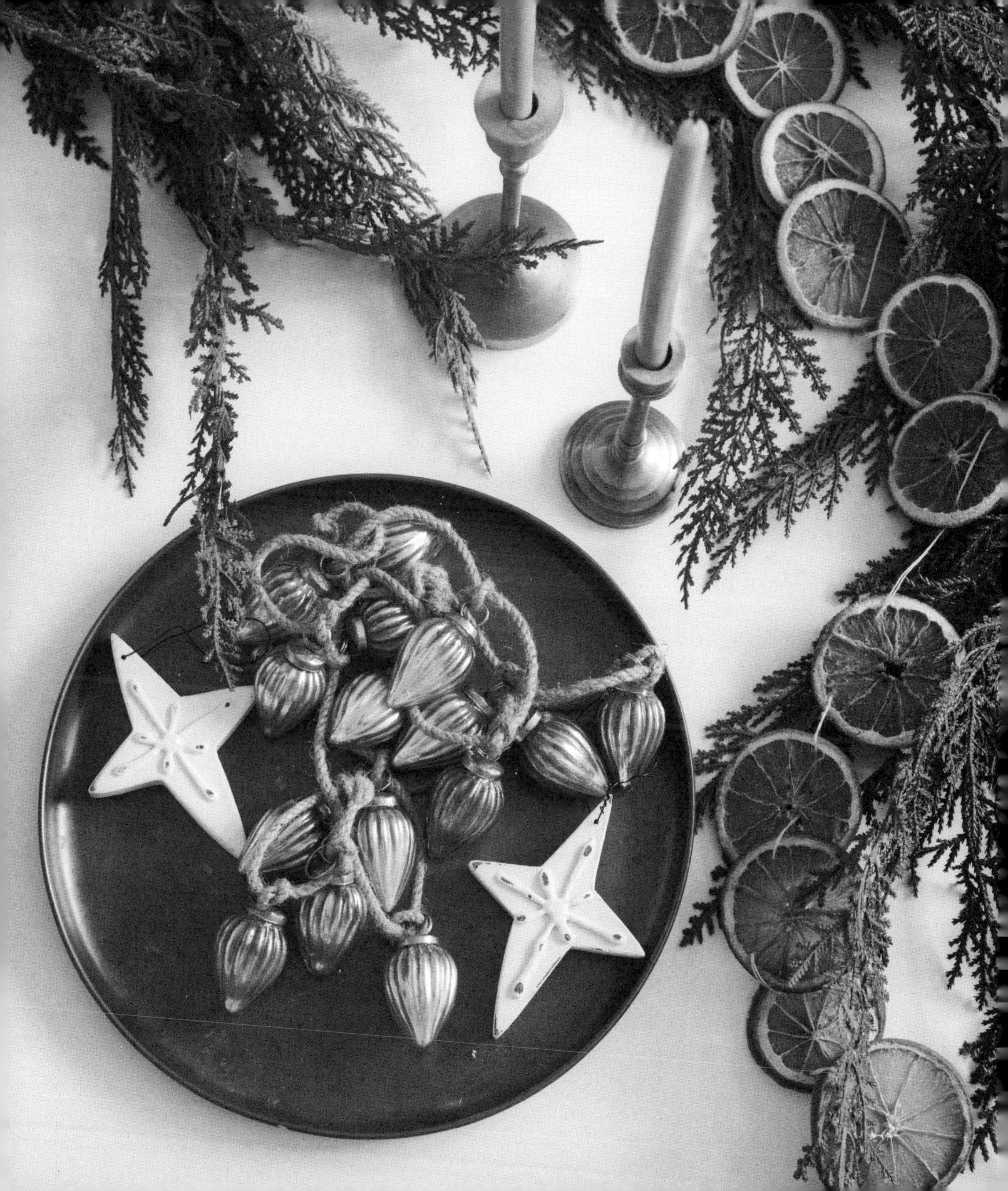

a votive candle at the door of every home in your neighborhood, or if that feels too adventurous, deliver them to just the neighbors on your street! As the darkest month of the year, December is a season of bringing light, no matter what religious background you come from. The spirit of light unites us and speaks to everyone. Invite your neighbors to light their candles at 5:00 p.m. on Christmas Eve and let them burn until the candle goes out. The light is a beautiful symbol of unity and peace. If the weather permits, you might take a candlelit walk through your neighborhood before everyone goes to bed for the night. This simple activity will be a beautiful and memorable reminder of this season of light. — INSPIRED BY KATIE AND EMILY

NEW YEAR'S EVE FONDUE NIGHT

On the very last night of the year, perhaps your family will gather to celebrate one final time. Consider hosting a family fondue night. Line up fondue pots down the center of the table, and fill them with olive oil. Perhaps you will spend the afternoon chopping up all the items you will cook for dinner that night. Some favorites include shrimp, steak, chicken, bacon, broccoli, cauliflower, sweet potatoes, mushrooms, zucchini, and brussels sprouts. You could also prepare a cheese fondue with different types of bread. Each of the different foods should be placed in small bowls and lined up next to the fondue pots. If your table is large, make sure there are two bowls of every food item, one for each end of the table.

It is easiest if everyone has their own colored skewers. You can purchase skewer sets with lots of different colors, or you can buy long wooden skewers and color the ends yourself. Set people's place settings with their colored skewers on top of their plates.

If you have never had fondue before, it's important to know that this dinner requires patience. Some people like to pick food items up one at a time, eating as they go, while others store up enough cooked food on their plates to eat their whole meal at once. A fondue night creates the perfect evening for laughing and eating and talking about all the good things in everyone's lives. Even little ones enjoy spending a slow evening eating together.

Once you are done with the dinner portion of the meal, clear all of the meat and vegetables off the table and bring over chocolate and caramel fondue with strawberries, cinnamon bears, marshmallows, clementines, apples, pretzels, cookies, or anything else that would taste good with chocolate on it. The conversations will continue, and everyone can enjoy being together. There is so much goodness here.

Having a fondue night or some other special dinner on New Year's Eve is one of the best ways to spend time while everyone is waiting up for midnight, because there is no rush. Time slows down, and all that matters is being together.

One of the things you might consider doing on this night is looking back through this gathering book, reading over your prayer list from each month. Not only will you be reminded of the things you petitioned Heavenly Father for throughout the year but you will also recall the miracles and tender mercies. The times when He answered. What would it be like to reflect over your most sacred moments as you look back? What would you learn? What would you remember? — INSPIRED BY EMILY

SEASONAL PLANNING PAGES CAN BE FOUND ON PAGE 233.

CHRISTMASTIME IS CHERISHED FAMILY TIME.
FAMILY TIME IS SACRED TIME.

Russell M. Nelson

PLANNING PAGES

THE SACRED IN THE EVERYDAY
52 sets of weekly worksheets

RITES OF PASSAGE
3 sets of planning worksheets

THE CELEBRATION OF SEASONS
12 sets of monthly worksheets

GENERAL CONFERENCE
2 sets of biannual worksheets

THE SACRED IN THE EVERYDAY

Week of
January 17

Create • Gather • Give

Prayer

AS A...	WHO OR WHAT ARE YOU **PRAYING** FOR?
mother	finding joy and satisfaction in being a mom
friend	that Jen will be sustained
friend	that I can connect w/ a broader swath of people
minister	understand how to connect
sister	that I can help A + M

Scripture

WHAT QUESTION WILL YOU TAKE TO THE SCRIPTURES?

What does God want me to do and be? Am I lacking something substantial

FAMILY **PROTECTION** SCRIPTURE:

Sabbath

HOW WILL YOU KEEP THE SABBATH THIS WEEK?

really pondering during the sacrament

HOW WILL YOU REMEMBER GOD & OTHERS?

- Facetime Reed
- talk to YW at church & text the rest

HOW CAN YOU CREATE MOMENTS OF TRADITION?

read scriptures with our guests

Mealtime

WHAT DAY THIS WEEK IS BEST FOR AN INTENTIONAL MEALTIME IN YOUR HOME?

MONDAY   TUESDAY   WEDNESDAY   THURSDAY   FRIDAY   SATURDAY   SUNDAY

HOW CAN YOU LIFT THE ONE?

Ollie has a lot on his plate with diabetes — have a special note from m & dad at his place

WHAT MOMENTS OF CELEBRATION OR CONNECTION CAN YOU CREATE DURING THIS TIME? HOW?

special keto dessert, maybe always have a homemade (healthy-ish) dessert on intentional dinner nights

Other Impressions

Week of
January 24

Create · Gather · Give

Prayer

AS A . . .

sister
mother
friend

WHO OR WHAT ARE YOU **PRAYING** FOR?

Megan's burden to be lifted
Ollie to be happy - diabetes
Who needs my invitation to the temple?

Scripture

WHAT QUESTION WILL YOU TAKE TO THE SCRIPTURES?

How can I reconnect with God every day?

FAMILY **PROTECTION** SCRIPTURE:

Sabbath

HOW WILL YOU KEEP THE SABBATH THIS WEEK?

perform an act of service

HOW WILL YOU REMEMBER GOD & OTHERS?

make calls to family we don't often call

HOW CAN YOU CREATE MOMENTS OF TRADITION?

Come, follow me lunch

Mealtime

WHAT DAY THIS WEEK IS BEST FOR AN INTENTIONAL MEALTIME IN YOUR HOME?

MONDAY   TUESDAY   (WEDNESDAY)   THURSDAY   FRIDAY   SATURDAY   SUNDAY

HOW CAN YOU LIFT THE ONE?

Ollie's favorites dinner

WHAT MOMENTS OF CELEBRATION OR CONNECTION CAN YOU CREATE DURING THIS TIME? HOW?

let him feel like his choices are important

Other Impressions

Week of

Create • Gather • Give

Prayer

AS A . . .

WHO OR WHAT ARE YOU **PRAYING** FOR?

Scripture

WHAT QUESTION WILL YOU TAKE TO THE SCRIPTURES?

FAMILY **PROTECTION** SCRIPTURE:

Sabbath

HOW WILL YOU **KEEP** THE SABBATH THIS WEEK?

_____

_____

_____

HOW WILL YOU **REMEMBER** GOD & OTHERS?

_____

_____

HOW CAN YOU CREATE MOMENTS OF TRADITION?

_____

_____

Mealtime

WHAT DAY THIS WEEK IS BEST FOR AN **INTENTIONAL** MEALTIME IN YOUR HOME?

MONDAY   TUESDAY   WEDNESDAY   THURSDAY   FRIDAY   SATURDAY   SUNDAY

HOW CAN YOU LIFT **THE ONE**?

_____

_____

WHAT MOMENTS OF CELEBRATION OR **CONNECTION** CAN YOU CREATE DURING THIS TIME? HOW?

_____

_____

Other Impressions

_____

_____

Week of

_____

Create • Gather • Give

Prayer

AS A . . .

_____
_____
_____
_____
_____
_____

WHO OR WHAT ARE YOU **PRAYING** FOR?

_____
_____
_____
_____
_____
_____

Scripture

WHAT QUESTION WILL YOU TAKE TO THE SCRIPTURES?

_____
_____
_____

FAMILY **PROTECTION** SCRIPTURE:

_____
_____
_____

Sabbath

HOW WILL YOU **KEEP** THE SABBATH THIS WEEK?

_____

_____

_____

HOW WILL YOU **REMEMBER** GOD & OTHERS?

_____

_____

_____

HOW CAN YOU CREATE MOMENTS OF TRADITION?

_____

_____

_____

Mealtime

WHAT DAY THIS WEEK IS BEST FOR AN **INTENTIONAL** MEALTIME IN YOUR HOME?

MONDAY   TUESDAY   WEDNESDAY   THURSDAY   FRIDAY   SATURDAY   SUNDAY

HOW CAN YOU LIFT **THE ONE**?

_____

_____

WHAT MOMENTS OF CELEBRATION OR **CONNECTION** CAN YOU CREATE DURING THIS TIME? HOW?

_____

_____

Other Impressions

_____

_____

Week of

Create • Gather • Give

Prayer

AS A . . .

WHO OR WHAT ARE YOU **PRAYING** FOR?

Scripture

WHAT QUESTION WILL YOU TAKE TO THE SCRIPTURES?

FAMILY **PROTECTION** SCRIPTURE:

Sabbath

HOW WILL YOU **KEEP** THE SABBATH THIS WEEK?

_____

_____

_____

HOW WILL YOU **REMEMBER** GOD & OTHERS?

_____

_____

_____

HOW CAN YOU CREATE MOMENTS OF TRADITION?

_____

_____

_____

Mealtime

WHAT DAY THIS WEEK IS BEST FOR AN **INTENTIONAL** MEALTIME IN YOUR HOME?

MONDAY   TUESDAY   WEDNESDAY   THURSDAY   FRIDAY   SATURDAY   SUNDAY

HOW CAN YOU LIFT **THE ONE**?

_____

_____

WHAT MOMENTS OF CELEBRATION OR **CONNECTION** CAN YOU CREATE DURING THIS TIME? HOW?

_____

_____

Other Impressions

_____

_____

Week of

_____

Create • Gather • Give

Prayer

AS A . . .

_____
_____
_____
_____
_____
_____

WHO OR WHAT ARE YOU **PRAYING** FOR?

_____
_____
_____
_____
_____
_____

Scripture

WHAT QUESTION WILL YOU TAKE TO THE SCRIPTURES?

_____
_____
_____
_____

FAMILY **PROTECTION** SCRIPTURE:

_____
_____
_____
_____

Sabbath

HOW WILL YOU **KEEP** THE SABBATH THIS WEEK?

_____

_____

_____

HOW WILL YOU **REMEMBER** GOD & OTHERS?

_____

_____

_____

HOW CAN YOU CREATE MOMENTS OF TRADITION?

_____

_____

_____

Mealtime

WHAT DAY THIS WEEK IS BEST FOR AN **INTENTIONAL** MEALTIME IN YOUR HOME?

MONDAY   TUESDAY   WEDNESDAY   THURSDAY   FRIDAY   SATURDAY   SUNDAY

HOW CAN YOU LIFT **THE ONE**?

_____

_____

WHAT MOMENTS OF CELEBRATION OR **CONNECTION** CAN YOU CREATE DURING THIS TIME? HOW?

_____

_____

Other Impressions

_____

_____

Week of

_____

Create • Gather • Give

Prayer

AS A . . .

_____
_____
_____
_____
_____
_____

WHO OR WHAT ARE YOU **PRAYING** FOR?

_____
_____
_____
_____
_____
_____

Scripture

WHAT QUESTION WILL YOU TAKE TO THE SCRIPTURES?

_____
_____
_____
_____

FAMILY **PROTECTION** SCRIPTURE:

_____
_____
_____

Sabbath

HOW WILL YOU **KEEP** THE SABBATH THIS WEEK?

_____

_____

_____

HOW WILL YOU **REMEMBER** GOD & OTHERS?

_____

_____

_____

HOW CAN YOU CREATE MOMENTS OF TRADITION?

_____

_____

_____

Mealtime

WHAT DAY THIS WEEK IS BEST FOR AN **INTENTIONAL** MEALTIME IN YOUR HOME?

MONDAY   TUESDAY   WEDNESDAY   THURSDAY   FRIDAY   SATURDAY   SUNDAY

HOW CAN YOU LIFT **THE ONE**?

_____

_____

WHAT MOMENTS OF CELEBRATION OR **CONNECTION** CAN YOU CREATE DURING THIS TIME? HOW?

_____

_____

Other Impressions

_____

_____

Week of

_____

Create • Gather • Give

Prayer

AS A . . .

_____
_____
_____
_____
_____
_____

WHO OR WHAT ARE YOU **PRAYING** FOR?

_____
_____
_____
_____
_____
_____

Scripture

WHAT QUESTION WILL YOU TAKE TO THE SCRIPTURES?

_____
_____
_____

FAMILY **PROTECTION** SCRIPTURE:

_____
_____
_____

Sabbath

HOW WILL YOU **KEEP** THE SABBATH THIS WEEK?

_____

_____

_____

HOW WILL YOU **REMEMBER** GOD & OTHERS?

_____

_____

_____

HOW CAN YOU CREATE MOMENTS OF TRADITION?

_____

_____

_____

Mealtime

WHAT DAY THIS WEEK IS BEST FOR AN **INTENTIONAL** MEALTIME IN YOUR HOME?

MONDAY   TUESDAY   WEDNESDAY   THURSDAY   FRIDAY   SATURDAY   SUNDAY

HOW CAN YOU LIFT **THE ONE**?

_____

_____

WHAT MOMENTS OF CELEBRATION OR **CONNECTION** CAN YOU CREATE DURING THIS TIME? HOW?

_____

_____

Other Impressions

_____

_____

Week of

Create • Gather • Give

Prayer

AS A . . .

WHO OR WHAT ARE YOU **PRAYING** FOR?

Scripture

WHAT QUESTION WILL YOU TAKE TO THE SCRIPTURES?

FAMILY **PROTECTION** SCRIPTURE:

Sabbath

HOW WILL YOU **KEEP** THE SABBATH THIS WEEK?

_____

_____

_____

HOW WILL YOU **REMEMBER** GOD & OTHERS?

_____

_____

_____

HOW CAN YOU CREATE MOMENTS OF TRADITION?

_____

_____

_____

Mealtime

WHAT DAY THIS WEEK IS BEST FOR AN **INTENTIONAL** MEALTIME IN YOUR HOME?

MONDAY   TUESDAY   WEDNESDAY   THURSDAY   FRIDAY   SATURDAY   SUNDAY

HOW CAN YOU LIFT **THE ONE**?

_____

_____

WHAT MOMENTS OF CELEBRATION OR **CONNECTION** CAN YOU CREATE DURING THIS TIME? HOW?

_____

_____

Other Impressions

_____

_____

Week of

_____

Create • Gather • Give

Prayer

AS A . . .

_____
_____
_____
_____
_____

WHO OR WHAT ARE YOU **PRAYING** FOR?

_____
_____
_____
_____
_____

Scripture

WHAT QUESTION WILL YOU TAKE TO THE SCRIPTURES?

_____
_____
_____
_____

FAMILY **PROTECTION** SCRIPTURE:

_____
_____
_____

Sabbath

HOW WILL YOU **KEEP** THE SABBATH THIS WEEK?

_____

_____

_____

HOW WILL YOU **REMEMBER** GOD & OTHERS?

_____

_____

_____

HOW CAN YOU CREATE MOMENTS OF TRADITION?

_____

_____

_____

Mealtime

WHAT DAY THIS WEEK IS BEST FOR AN **INTENTIONAL** MEALTIME IN YOUR HOME?

MONDAY   TUESDAY   WEDNESDAY   THURSDAY   FRIDAY   SATURDAY   SUNDAY

HOW CAN YOU LIFT **THE ONE**?

_____

_____

WHAT MOMENTS OF CELEBRATION OR **CONNECTION** CAN YOU CREATE DURING THIS TIME? HOW?

_____

_____

Other Impressions

_____

_____

Week of

_____

Create · Gather · Give

Prayer

AS A . . .

_____
_____
_____
_____
_____
_____

WHO OR WHAT ARE YOU **PRAYING** FOR?

_____
_____
_____
_____
_____
_____

Scripture

WHAT QUESTION WILL YOU TAKE TO THE SCRIPTURES?

_____
_____
_____
_____

FAMILY **PROTECTION** SCRIPTURE:

_____
_____
_____
_____

Sabbath

HOW WILL YOU **KEEP** THE SABBATH THIS WEEK?

_____

_____

_____

HOW WILL YOU **REMEMBER** GOD & OTHERS?

_____

_____

_____

HOW CAN YOU CREATE MOMENTS OF TRADITION?

_____

_____

_____

Mealtime

WHAT DAY THIS WEEK IS BEST FOR AN **INTENTIONAL** MEALTIME IN YOUR HOME?

MONDAY   TUESDAY   WEDNESDAY   THURSDAY   FRIDAY   SATURDAY   SUNDAY

HOW CAN YOU LIFT **THE ONE**?

_____

_____

WHAT MOMENTS OF CELEBRATION OR **CONNECTION** CAN YOU CREATE DURING THIS TIME? HOW?

_____

_____

Other Impressions

_____

_____

Week of

Create • Gather • Give

Prayer

AS A . . .

WHO OR WHAT ARE YOU **PRAYING** FOR?

Scripture

WHAT QUESTION WILL YOU TAKE TO THE SCRIPTURES?

FAMILY **PROTECTION** SCRIPTURE:

Sabbath

HOW WILL YOU **KEEP** THE SABBATH THIS WEEK?

_____

_____

_____

HOW WILL YOU **REMEMBER** GOD & OTHERS?

_____

_____

_____

HOW CAN YOU CREATE MOMENTS OF TRADITION?

_____

_____

_____

Mealtime

WHAT DAY THIS WEEK IS BEST FOR AN **INTENTIONAL** MEALTIME IN YOUR HOME?

MONDAY   TUESDAY   WEDNESDAY   THURSDAY   FRIDAY   SATURDAY   SUNDAY

HOW CAN YOU LIFT **THE ONE**?

_____

_____

WHAT MOMENTS OF CELEBRATION OR **CONNECTION** CAN YOU CREATE DURING THIS TIME? HOW?

_____

_____

Other Impressions

_____

_____

Week of

_____

Create • Gather • Give

Prayer

AS A . . .

_____
_____
_____
_____
_____
_____

WHO OR WHAT ARE YOU **PRAYING** FOR?

_____
_____
_____
_____
_____
_____

Scripture

WHAT QUESTION WILL YOU TAKE TO THE SCRIPTURES?

_____
_____
_____
_____

FAMILY **PROTECTION** SCRIPTURE:

_____
_____
_____

Sabbath

HOW WILL YOU **KEEP** THE SABBATH THIS WEEK?

_____

_____

_____

HOW WILL YOU **REMEMBER** GOD & OTHERS?

_____

_____

_____

HOW CAN YOU CREATE MOMENTS OF TRADITION?

_____

_____

_____

Mealtime

WHAT DAY THIS WEEK IS BEST FOR AN **INTENTIONAL** MEALTIME IN YOUR HOME?

MONDAY   TUESDAY   WEDNESDAY   THURSDAY   FRIDAY   SATURDAY   SUNDAY

HOW CAN YOU LIFT **THE ONE**?

_____

_____

WHAT MOMENTS OF CELEBRATION OR **CONNECTION** CAN YOU CREATE DURING THIS TIME? HOW?

_____

_____

Other Impressions

_____

_____

Week of

_____

Create • Gather • Give

Prayer

AS A . . .

_____
_____
_____
_____
_____
_____

WHO OR WHAT ARE YOU **PRAYING** FOR?

_____
_____
_____
_____
_____
_____

Scripture

WHAT QUESTION WILL YOU TAKE TO THE SCRIPTURES?

_____
_____
_____
_____

FAMILY **PROTECTION** SCRIPTURE:

_____
_____
_____
_____

Sabbath

HOW WILL YOU **KEEP** THE SABBATH THIS WEEK?

_____

_____

_____

HOW WILL YOU **REMEMBER** GOD & OTHERS?

_____

_____

_____

HOW CAN YOU CREATE MOMENTS OF TRADITION?

_____

_____

_____

Mealtime

WHAT DAY THIS WEEK IS BEST FOR AN **INTENTIONAL** MEALTIME IN YOUR HOME?

MONDAY   TUESDAY   WEDNESDAY   THURSDAY   FRIDAY   SATURDAY   SUNDAY

HOW CAN YOU LIFT **THE ONE**?

_____

_____

WHAT MOMENTS OF CELEBRATION OR **CONNECTION** CAN YOU CREATE DURING THIS TIME? HOW?

_____

_____

Other Impressions

_____

_____

Week of

_____

Create · Gather · Give

Prayer

AS A . . .

_____
_____
_____
_____
_____

WHO OR WHAT ARE YOU **PRAYING** FOR?

_____
_____
_____
_____
_____

Scripture

WHAT QUESTION WILL YOU TAKE TO THE SCRIPTURES?

_____
_____
_____
_____

FAMILY **PROTECTION** SCRIPTURE:

_____
_____
_____

Sabbath

HOW WILL YOU **KEEP** THE SABBATH THIS WEEK?

_____

_____

_____

HOW WILL YOU **REMEMBER** GOD & OTHERS?

_____

_____

_____

HOW CAN YOU CREATE MOMENTS OF TRADITION?

_____

_____

_____

Mealtime

WHAT DAY THIS WEEK IS BEST FOR AN **INTENTIONAL** MEALTIME IN YOUR HOME?

MONDAY   TUESDAY   WEDNESDAY   THURSDAY   FRIDAY   SATURDAY   SUNDAY

HOW CAN YOU LIFT **THE ONE**?

_____

_____

WHAT MOMENTS OF CELEBRATION OR **CONNECTION** CAN YOU CREATE DURING THIS TIME? HOW?

_____

_____

Other Impressions

_____

_____

Week of

_____

Create • Gather • Give

Prayer

AS A . . .

_____
_____
_____
_____
_____
_____

WHO OR WHAT ARE YOU **PRAYING** FOR?

_____
_____
_____
_____
_____
_____

Scripture

WHAT QUESTION WILL YOU TAKE TO THE SCRIPTURES?

_____
_____
_____
_____

FAMILY **PROTECTION** SCRIPTURE:

_____
_____
_____
_____

Sabbath

HOW WILL YOU **KEEP** THE SABBATH THIS WEEK?

_____

_____

_____

HOW WILL YOU **REMEMBER** GOD & OTHERS?

_____

_____

_____

HOW CAN YOU CREATE MOMENTS OF TRADITION?

_____

_____

_____

Mealtime

WHAT DAY THIS WEEK IS BEST FOR AN **INTENTIONAL** MEALTIME IN YOUR HOME?

MONDAY   TUESDAY   WEDNESDAY   THURSDAY   FRIDAY   SATURDAY   SUNDAY

HOW CAN YOU LIFT **THE ONE**?

_____

_____

WHAT MOMENTS OF CELEBRATION OR **CONNECTION** CAN YOU CREATE DURING THIS TIME? HOW?

_____

_____

Other Impressions

_____

_____

Week of

_____

Create • Gather • Give

Prayer

AS A . . .

_____
_____
_____
_____
_____

WHO OR WHAT ARE YOU **PRAYING** FOR?

_____
_____
_____
_____
_____

Scripture

WHAT QUESTION WILL YOU TAKE TO THE SCRIPTURES?

_____
_____
_____

FAMILY **PROTECTION** SCRIPTURE:

_____
_____
_____

Sabbath

HOW WILL YOU **KEEP** THE SABBATH THIS WEEK?

_____

_____

_____

HOW WILL YOU **REMEMBER** GOD & OTHERS?

_____

_____

_____

HOW CAN YOU CREATE MOMENTS OF TRADITION?

_____

_____

_____

Mealtime

WHAT DAY THIS WEEK IS BEST FOR AN **INTENTIONAL** MEALTIME IN YOUR HOME?

MONDAY   TUESDAY   WEDNESDAY   THURSDAY   FRIDAY   SATURDAY   SUNDAY

HOW CAN YOU LIFT **THE ONE**?

_____

_____

WHAT MOMENTS OF CELEBRATION OR **CONNECTION** CAN YOU CREATE DURING THIS TIME? HOW?

_____

_____

Other Impressions

_____

_____

Week of

_____

Create • Gather • Give

Prayer

AS A . . .

_____
_____
_____
_____
_____
_____

WHO OR WHAT ARE YOU **PRAYING** FOR?

_____
_____
_____
_____
_____
_____

Scripture

WHAT QUESTION WILL YOU TAKE TO THE SCRIPTURES?

_____
_____
_____
_____

FAMILY **PROTECTION** SCRIPTURE:

_____
_____
_____
_____

Sabbath

HOW WILL YOU **KEEP** THE SABBATH THIS WEEK?

_____

_____

_____

HOW WILL YOU **REMEMBER** GOD & OTHERS?

_____

_____

_____

HOW CAN YOU CREATE MOMENTS OF TRADITION?

_____

_____

_____

Mealtime

WHAT DAY THIS WEEK IS BEST FOR AN **INTENTIONAL** MEALTIME IN YOUR HOME?

MONDAY   TUESDAY   WEDNESDAY   THURSDAY   FRIDAY   SATURDAY   SUNDAY

HOW CAN YOU LIFT **THE ONE**?

_____

_____

_____

WHAT MOMENTS OF CELEBRATION OR **CONNECTION** CAN YOU CREATE DURING THIS TIME? HOW?

_____

_____

_____

Other Impressions

_____

_____

Week of

_____

Create • Gather • Give

Prayer

AS A . . .

_____
_____
_____
_____
_____
_____

WHO OR WHAT ARE YOU **PRAYING** FOR?

_____
_____
_____
_____
_____
_____

Scripture

WHAT QUESTION WILL YOU TAKE TO THE SCRIPTURES?

_____
_____
_____
_____

FAMILY **PROTECTION** SCRIPTURE:

_____
_____
_____

Sabbath

HOW WILL YOU **KEEP** THE SABBATH THIS WEEK?

_____

_____

_____

HOW WILL YOU **REMEMBER** GOD & OTHERS?

_____

_____

_____

HOW CAN YOU CREATE MOMENTS OF TRADITION?

_____

_____

_____

Mealtime

WHAT DAY THIS WEEK IS BEST FOR AN **INTENTIONAL** MEALTIME IN YOUR HOME?

MONDAY   TUESDAY   WEDNESDAY   THURSDAY   FRIDAY   SATURDAY   SUNDAY

HOW CAN YOU LIFT **THE ONE**?

_____

_____

WHAT MOMENTS OF CELEBRATION OR **CONNECTION** CAN YOU CREATE DURING THIS TIME? HOW?

_____

_____

Other Impressions

_____

_____

Week of

Create • Gather • Give

Prayer

AS A . . .

WHO OR WHAT ARE YOU **PRAYING** FOR?

Scripture

WHAT QUESTION WILL YOU TAKE TO THE SCRIPTURES?

FAMILY **PROTECTION** SCRIPTURE:

Sabbath

HOW WILL YOU **KEEP** THE SABBATH THIS WEEK?

_____

_____

_____

HOW WILL YOU **REMEMBER** GOD & OTHERS?

_____

_____

_____

HOW CAN YOU CREATE MOMENTS OF TRADITION?

_____

_____

_____

Mealtime

WHAT DAY THIS WEEK IS BEST FOR AN **INTENTIONAL** MEALTIME IN YOUR HOME?

MONDAY   TUESDAY   WEDNESDAY   THURSDAY   FRIDAY   SATURDAY   SUNDAY

HOW CAN YOU LIFT **THE ONE**?

_____

_____

WHAT MOMENTS OF CELEBRATION OR **CONNECTION** CAN YOU CREATE DURING THIS TIME? HOW?

_____

_____

Other Impressions

_____

_____

Week of

_____

Create • Gather • Give

Prayer

AS A . . .

_____
_____
_____
_____
_____
_____

WHO OR WHAT ARE YOU **PRAYING** FOR?

_____
_____
_____
_____
_____
_____

Scripture

WHAT QUESTION WILL YOU TAKE TO THE SCRIPTURES?

_____
_____
_____
_____

FAMILY **PROTECTION** SCRIPTURE:

_____
_____
_____

Sabbath

HOW WILL YOU **KEEP** THE SABBATH THIS WEEK?

_____

_____

_____

HOW WILL YOU **REMEMBER** GOD & OTHERS?

_____

_____

_____

HOW CAN YOU CREATE MOMENTS OF TRADITION?

_____

_____

_____

Mealtime

WHAT DAY THIS WEEK IS BEST FOR AN **INTENTIONAL** MEALTIME IN YOUR HOME?

MONDAY   TUESDAY   WEDNESDAY   THURSDAY   FRIDAY   SATURDAY   SUNDAY

HOW CAN YOU LIFT **THE ONE**?

_____

_____

WHAT MOMENTS OF CELEBRATION OR **CONNECTION** CAN YOU CREATE DURING THIS TIME? HOW?

_____

_____

Other Impressions

_____

_____

Week of

_____

Create • Gather • Give

Prayer

AS A . . .

_____
_____
_____
_____
_____
_____

WHO OR WHAT ARE YOU **PRAYING** FOR?

_____
_____
_____
_____
_____
_____

Scripture

WHAT QUESTION WILL YOU TAKE TO THE SCRIPTURES?

_____
_____
_____
_____

FAMILY **PROTECTION** SCRIPTURE:

_____
_____
_____

Sabbath

HOW WILL YOU **KEEP** THE SABBATH THIS WEEK?

_____

_____

_____

HOW WILL YOU **REMEMBER** GOD & OTHERS?

_____

_____

_____

HOW CAN YOU CREATE MOMENTS OF TRADITION?

_____

_____

_____

Mealtime

WHAT DAY THIS WEEK IS BEST FOR AN **INTENTIONAL** MEALTIME IN YOUR HOME?

MONDAY   TUESDAY   WEDNESDAY   THURSDAY   FRIDAY   SATURDAY   SUNDAY

HOW CAN YOU LIFT **THE ONE**?

_____

_____

WHAT MOMENTS OF CELEBRATION OR **CONNECTION** CAN YOU CREATE DURING THIS TIME? HOW?

_____

_____

Other Impressions

_____

_____

Week of

Create • Gather • Give

Prayer

AS A . . .

WHO OR WHAT ARE YOU **PRAYING** FOR?

Scripture

WHAT QUESTION WILL YOU TAKE TO THE SCRIPTURES?

FAMILY **PROTECTION** SCRIPTURE:

Sabbath

HOW WILL YOU **KEEP** THE SABBATH THIS WEEK?

_____

_____

_____

HOW WILL YOU **REMEMBER** GOD & OTHERS?

_____

_____

_____

HOW CAN YOU CREATE MOMENTS OF TRADITION?

_____

_____

_____

Mealtime

WHAT DAY THIS WEEK IS BEST FOR AN **INTENTIONAL** MEALTIME IN YOUR HOME?

MONDAY   TUESDAY   WEDNESDAY   THURSDAY   FRIDAY   SATURDAY   SUNDAY

HOW CAN YOU LIFT **THE ONE**?

_____

_____

WHAT MOMENTS OF CELEBRATION OR **CONNECTION** CAN YOU CREATE DURING THIS TIME? HOW?

_____

_____

Other Impressions

_____

_____

Week of

_____

Create • Gather • Give

Prayer

AS A . . .

_____
_____
_____
_____
_____
_____

WHO OR WHAT ARE YOU **PRAYING** FOR?

_____
_____
_____
_____
_____
_____

Scripture

WHAT QUESTION WILL YOU TAKE TO THE SCRIPTURES?

_____
_____
_____
_____

FAMILY **PROTECTION** SCRIPTURE:

_____
_____
_____
_____

Sabbath

HOW WILL YOU **KEEP** THE SABBATH THIS WEEK?

_____

_____

_____

HOW WILL YOU **REMEMBER** GOD & OTHERS?

_____

_____

_____

HOW CAN YOU CREATE MOMENTS OF TRADITION?

_____

_____

_____

Mealtime

WHAT DAY THIS WEEK IS BEST FOR AN **INTENTIONAL** MEALTIME IN YOUR HOME?

MONDAY   TUESDAY   WEDNESDAY   THURSDAY   FRIDAY   SATURDAY   SUNDAY

HOW CAN YOU LIFT **THE ONE**?

_____

_____

WHAT MOMENTS OF CELEBRATION OR **CONNECTION** CAN YOU CREATE DURING THIS TIME? HOW?

_____

_____

Other Impressions

_____

_____

Week of

_____

Create • Gather • Give

Prayer

AS A . . .

_____
_____
_____
_____
_____
_____

WHO OR WHAT ARE YOU **PRAYING** FOR?

_____
_____
_____
_____
_____
_____

Scripture

WHAT QUESTION WILL YOU TAKE TO THE SCRIPTURES?

_____
_____
_____

FAMILY **PROTECTION** SCRIPTURE:

_____
_____
_____

Sabbath

HOW WILL YOU **KEEP** THE SABBATH THIS WEEK?

_____

_____

_____

HOW WILL YOU **REMEMBER** GOD & OTHERS?

_____

_____

_____

HOW CAN YOU CREATE MOMENTS OF TRADITION?

_____

_____

_____

Mealtime

WHAT DAY THIS WEEK IS BEST FOR AN **INTENTIONAL** MEALTIME IN YOUR HOME?

MONDAY   TUESDAY   WEDNESDAY   THURSDAY   FRIDAY   SATURDAY   SUNDAY

HOW CAN YOU LIFT **THE ONE**?

_____

_____

WHAT MOMENTS OF CELEBRATION OR **CONNECTION** CAN YOU CREATE DURING THIS TIME? HOW?

_____

_____

Other Impressions

_____

_____

Week of

_____

Create · Gather · Give

Prayer

AS A . . .

_____
_____
_____
_____
_____

WHO OR WHAT ARE YOU **PRAYING** FOR?

_____
_____
_____
_____
_____

Scripture

WHAT QUESTION WILL YOU TAKE TO THE SCRIPTURES?

_____
_____
_____

FAMILY **PROTECTION** SCRIPTURE:

_____
_____
_____

Sabbath

HOW WILL YOU **KEEP** THE SABBATH THIS WEEK?

HOW WILL YOU **REMEMBER** GOD & OTHERS?

HOW CAN YOU CREATE MOMENTS OF TRADITION?

Mealtime

WHAT DAY THIS WEEK IS BEST FOR AN **INTENTIONAL** MEALTIME IN YOUR HOME?

MONDAY   TUESDAY   WEDNESDAY   THURSDAY   FRIDAY   SATURDAY   SUNDAY

HOW CAN YOU LIFT **THE ONE**?

WHAT MOMENTS OF CELEBRATION OR **CONNECTION** CAN YOU CREATE DURING THIS TIME? HOW?

Other Impressions

Week of

Create • Gather • Give

Prayer

AS A . . .

WHO OR WHAT ARE YOU **PRAYING** FOR?

Scripture

WHAT QUESTION WILL YOU TAKE TO THE SCRIPTURES?

FAMILY **PROTECTION** SCRIPTURE:

Sabbath

HOW WILL YOU **KEEP** THE SABBATH THIS WEEK?

_____

_____

_____

HOW WILL YOU **REMEMBER** GOD & OTHERS?

_____

_____

_____

HOW CAN YOU CREATE MOMENTS OF TRADITION?

_____

_____

_____

Mealtime

WHAT DAY THIS WEEK IS BEST FOR AN **INTENTIONAL** MEALTIME IN YOUR HOME?

MONDAY   TUESDAY   WEDNESDAY   THURSDAY   FRIDAY   SATURDAY   SUNDAY

HOW CAN YOU LIFT **THE ONE**?

_____

_____

WHAT MOMENTS OF CELEBRATION OR **CONNECTION** CAN YOU CREATE DURING THIS TIME? HOW?

_____

_____

Other Impressions

_____

_____

Week of

_____

Create • Gather • Give

Prayer

AS A . . .

_____
_____
_____
_____
_____
_____

WHO OR WHAT ARE YOU **PRAYING** FOR?

_____
_____
_____
_____
_____
_____

Scripture

WHAT QUESTION WILL YOU TAKE TO THE SCRIPTURES?

_____
_____
_____
_____

FAMILY **PROTECTION** SCRIPTURE:

_____
_____
_____

Sabbath

HOW WILL YOU **KEEP** THE SABBATH THIS WEEK?

HOW WILL YOU **REMEMBER** GOD & OTHERS?

HOW CAN YOU CREATE MOMENTS OF TRADITION?

Mealtime

WHAT DAY THIS WEEK IS BEST FOR AN **INTENTIONAL** MEALTIME IN YOUR HOME?

MONDAY   TUESDAY   WEDNESDAY   THURSDAY   FRIDAY   SATURDAY   SUNDAY

HOW CAN YOU LIFT **THE ONE**?

WHAT MOMENTS OF CELEBRATION OR **CONNECTION** CAN YOU CREATE DURING THIS TIME? HOW?

Other Impressions

Week of

Create • Gather • Give

_____

Prayer

AS A . . .

WHO OR WHAT ARE YOU **PRAYING** FOR?

Scripture

WHAT QUESTION WILL YOU TAKE TO THE SCRIPTURES?

FAMILY **PROTECTION** SCRIPTURE:

Sabbath

HOW WILL YOU **KEEP** THE SABBATH THIS WEEK?

_____

_____

_____

HOW WILL YOU **REMEMBER** GOD & OTHERS?

_____

_____

_____

HOW CAN YOU CREATE MOMENTS OF TRADITION?

_____

_____

_____

Mealtime

WHAT DAY THIS WEEK IS BEST FOR AN **INTENTIONAL** MEALTIME IN YOUR HOME?

MONDAY TUESDAY WEDNESDAY THURSDAY FRIDAY SATURDAY SUNDAY

HOW CAN YOU LIFT **THE ONE**?

_____

_____

WHAT MOMENTS OF CELEBRATION OR **CONNECTION** CAN YOU CREATE DURING THIS TIME? HOW?

_____

_____

Other Impressions

_____

_____

Week of

_____

Create • Gather • Give

Prayer

AS A . . .

WHO OR WHAT ARE YOU **PRAYING** FOR?

Scripture

WHAT QUESTION WILL YOU TAKE TO THE SCRIPTURES?

FAMILY **PROTECTION** SCRIPTURE:

Sabbath

HOW WILL YOU **KEEP** THE SABBATH THIS WEEK?

_____

_____

HOW WILL YOU **REMEMBER** GOD & OTHERS?

_____

_____

HOW CAN YOU CREATE MOMENTS OF TRADITION?

_____

_____

Mealtime

WHAT DAY THIS WEEK IS BEST FOR AN **INTENTIONAL** MEALTIME IN YOUR HOME?

MONDAY   TUESDAY   WEDNESDAY   THURSDAY   FRIDAY   SATURDAY   SUNDAY

HOW CAN YOU LIFT **THE ONE**?

_____

_____

WHAT MOMENTS OF CELEBRATION OR **CONNECTION** CAN YOU CREATE DURING THIS TIME? HOW?

_____

_____

Other Impressions

_____

_____

Week of

_____

Create • Gather • Give

Prayer

AS A . . .

WHO OR WHAT ARE YOU **PRAYING** FOR?

Scripture

WHAT QUESTION WILL YOU TAKE TO THE SCRIPTURES?

FAMILY **PROTECTION** SCRIPTURE:

Sabbath

HOW WILL YOU **KEEP** THE SABBATH THIS WEEK?

_____

_____

_____

HOW WILL YOU **REMEMBER** GOD & OTHERS?

_____

_____

_____

HOW CAN YOU CREATE MOMENTS OF TRADITION?

_____

_____

_____

Mealtime

WHAT DAY THIS WEEK IS BEST FOR AN **INTENTIONAL** MEALTIME IN YOUR HOME?

MONDAY   TUESDAY   WEDNESDAY   THURSDAY   FRIDAY   SATURDAY   SUNDAY

HOW CAN YOU LIFT **THE ONE**?

_____

_____

WHAT MOMENTS OF CELEBRATION OR **CONNECTION** CAN YOU CREATE DURING THIS TIME? HOW?

_____

_____

Other Impressions

_____

_____

Week of

_____

Create • Gather • Give

Prayer

AS A . . .

_____
_____
_____
_____
_____
_____

WHO OR WHAT ARE YOU **PRAYING** FOR?

_____
_____
_____
_____
_____
_____

Scripture

WHAT QUESTION WILL YOU TAKE TO THE SCRIPTURES?

_____
_____
_____

FAMILY **PROTECTION** SCRIPTURE:

_____
_____
_____

Sabbath

HOW WILL YOU **KEEP** THE SABBATH THIS WEEK?

_____

_____

_____

HOW WILL YOU **REMEMBER** GOD & OTHERS?

_____

_____

_____

HOW CAN YOU CREATE MOMENTS OF TRADITION?

_____

_____

_____

Mealtime

WHAT DAY THIS WEEK IS BEST FOR AN **INTENTIONAL** MEALTIME IN YOUR HOME?

MONDAY   TUESDAY   WEDNESDAY   THURSDAY   FRIDAY   SATURDAY   SUNDAY

HOW CAN YOU LIFT **THE ONE**?

_____

_____

WHAT MOMENTS OF CELEBRATION OR **CONNECTION** CAN YOU CREATE DURING THIS TIME? HOW?

_____

_____

Other Impressions

_____

_____

Week of

_____

Create • Gather • Give

Prayer

AS A . . .

_____
_____
_____
_____
_____
_____

WHO OR WHAT ARE YOU **PRAYING** FOR?

_____
_____
_____
_____
_____
_____

Scripture

WHAT QUESTION WILL YOU TAKE TO THE SCRIPTURES?

_____
_____
_____
_____

FAMILY **PROTECTION** SCRIPTURE:

_____
_____
_____
_____

Sabbath

HOW WILL YOU **KEEP** THE SABBATH THIS WEEK?

_____

_____

_____

HOW WILL YOU **REMEMBER** GOD & OTHERS?

_____

_____

_____

HOW CAN YOU CREATE MOMENTS OF TRADITION?

_____

_____

_____

Mealtime

WHAT DAY THIS WEEK IS BEST FOR AN **INTENTIONAL** MEALTIME IN YOUR HOME?

MONDAY   TUESDAY   WEDNESDAY   THURSDAY   FRIDAY   SATURDAY   SUNDAY

HOW CAN YOU LIFT **THE ONE**?

_____

_____

WHAT MOMENTS OF CELEBRATION OR **CONNECTION** CAN YOU CREATE DURING THIS TIME? HOW?

_____

_____

Other Impressions

_____

_____

Week of

_____

Create • Gather • Give

Prayer

AS A . . .

_____
_____
_____
_____
_____
_____

WHO OR WHAT ARE YOU **PRAYING** FOR?

_____
_____
_____
_____
_____
_____

Scripture

WHAT QUESTION WILL YOU TAKE TO THE SCRIPTURES?

_____
_____
_____
_____

FAMILY **PROTECTION** SCRIPTURE:

_____
_____
_____

Sabbath

HOW WILL YOU **KEEP** THE SABBATH THIS WEEK?

HOW WILL YOU **REMEMBER** GOD & OTHERS?

HOW CAN YOU CREATE MOMENTS OF TRADITION?

Mealtime

WHAT DAY THIS WEEK IS BEST FOR AN **INTENTIONAL** MEALTIME IN YOUR HOME?

MONDAY   TUESDAY   WEDNESDAY   THURSDAY   FRIDAY   SATURDAY   SUNDAY

HOW CAN YOU LIFT **THE ONE**?

WHAT MOMENTS OF CELEBRATION OR **CONNECTION** CAN YOU CREATE DURING THIS TIME? HOW?

Other Impressions

Week of

_____

Create • Gather • Give

Prayer

AS A . . .

WHO OR WHAT ARE YOU **PRAYING** FOR?

Scripture

WHAT QUESTION WILL YOU TAKE TO THE SCRIPTURES?

FAMILY **PROTECTION** SCRIPTURE:

Sabbath

HOW WILL YOU **KEEP** THE SABBATH THIS WEEK?

_____

_____

_____

HOW WILL YOU **REMEMBER** GOD & OTHERS?

_____

_____

_____

HOW CAN YOU CREATE MOMENTS OF TRADITION?

_____

_____

_____

Mealtime

WHAT DAY THIS WEEK IS BEST FOR AN **INTENTIONAL** MEALTIME IN YOUR HOME?

MONDAY   TUESDAY   WEDNESDAY   THURSDAY   FRIDAY   SATURDAY   SUNDAY

HOW CAN YOU LIFT **THE ONE**?

_____

_____

WHAT MOMENTS OF CELEBRATION OR **CONNECTION** CAN YOU CREATE DURING THIS TIME? HOW?

_____

_____

Other Impressions

_____

_____

Week of

Create • Gather • Give

Prayer

AS A . . .

WHO OR WHAT ARE YOU **PRAYING** FOR?

Scripture

WHAT QUESTION WILL YOU TAKE TO THE SCRIPTURES?

FAMILY **PROTECTION** SCRIPTURE:

Sabbath

HOW WILL YOU **KEEP** THE SABBATH THIS WEEK?

_____

_____

_____

HOW WILL YOU **REMEMBER** GOD & OTHERS?

_____

_____

_____

HOW CAN YOU CREATE MOMENTS OF TRADITION?

_____

_____

_____

Mealtime

WHAT DAY THIS WEEK IS BEST FOR AN **INTENTIONAL** MEALTIME IN YOUR HOME?

MONDAY   TUESDAY   WEDNESDAY   THURSDAY   FRIDAY   SATURDAY   SUNDAY

HOW CAN YOU LIFT **THE ONE**?

_____

_____

WHAT MOMENTS OF CELEBRATION OR **CONNECTION** CAN YOU CREATE DURING THIS TIME? HOW?

_____

_____

Other Impressions

_____

_____

Week of

_____

Create • Gather • Give

Prayer

AS A . . .

_____
_____
_____
_____
_____
_____

WHO OR WHAT ARE YOU **PRAYING** FOR?

_____
_____
_____
_____
_____
_____

Scripture

WHAT QUESTION WILL YOU TAKE TO THE SCRIPTURES?

_____
_____
_____

FAMILY **PROTECTION** SCRIPTURE:

_____
_____
_____

Sabbath

HOW WILL YOU **KEEP** THE SABBATH THIS WEEK?

_____

_____

_____

HOW WILL YOU **REMEMBER** GOD & OTHERS?

_____

_____

_____

HOW CAN YOU CREATE MOMENTS OF TRADITION?

_____

_____

_____

Mealtime

WHAT DAY THIS WEEK IS BEST FOR AN **INTENTIONAL** MEALTIME IN YOUR HOME?

MONDAY   TUESDAY   WEDNESDAY   THURSDAY   FRIDAY   SATURDAY   SUNDAY

HOW CAN YOU LIFT **THE ONE**?

_____

_____

WHAT MOMENTS OF CELEBRATION OR **CONNECTION** CAN YOU CREATE DURING THIS TIME? HOW?

_____

_____

Other Impressions

_____

_____

Week of

_____

Create • Gather • Give

Prayer

AS A . . .

_____
_____
_____
_____
_____
_____

WHO OR WHAT ARE YOU **PRAYING** FOR?

_____
_____
_____
_____
_____
_____

Scripture

WHAT QUESTION WILL YOU TAKE TO THE SCRIPTURES?

_____
_____
_____
_____

FAMILY **PROTECTION** SCRIPTURE:

_____
_____
_____
_____

Sabbath

HOW WILL YOU **KEEP** THE SABBATH THIS WEEK?

_____

_____

_____

HOW WILL YOU **REMEMBER** GOD & OTHERS?

_____

_____

_____

HOW CAN YOU CREATE MOMENTS OF TRADITION?

_____

_____

_____

Mealtime

WHAT DAY THIS WEEK IS BEST FOR AN **INTENTIONAL** MEALTIME IN YOUR HOME?

MONDAY   TUESDAY   WEDNESDAY   THURSDAY   FRIDAY   SATURDAY   SUNDAY

HOW CAN YOU LIFT **THE ONE**?

_____

_____

WHAT MOMENTS OF CELEBRATION OR **CONNECTION** CAN YOU CREATE DURING THIS TIME? HOW?

_____

_____

Other Impressions

_____

_____

Week of

_____

Create • Gather • Give

Prayer

AS A . . .

_____
_____
_____
_____
_____
_____

WHO OR WHAT ARE YOU **PRAYING** FOR?

_____
_____
_____
_____
_____
_____

Scripture

WHAT QUESTION WILL YOU TAKE TO THE SCRIPTURES?

_____
_____
_____
_____

FAMILY **PROTECTION** SCRIPTURE:

_____
_____
_____
_____

Sabbath

HOW WILL YOU **KEEP** THE SABBATH THIS WEEK?

_____

_____

_____

HOW WILL YOU **REMEMBER** GOD & OTHERS?

_____

_____

_____

HOW CAN YOU CREATE MOMENTS OF TRADITION?

_____

_____

_____

Mealtime

WHAT DAY THIS WEEK IS BEST FOR AN **INTENTIONAL** MEALTIME IN YOUR HOME?

MONDAY   TUESDAY   WEDNESDAY   THURSDAY   FRIDAY   SATURDAY   SUNDAY

HOW CAN YOU LIFT **THE ONE**?

_____

_____

WHAT MOMENTS OF CELEBRATION OR **CONNECTION** CAN YOU CREATE DURING THIS TIME? HOW?

_____

_____

Other Impressions

_____

_____

Week of

_____

Create • Gather • Give

Prayer

AS A . . .

_____
_____
_____
_____
_____
_____

WHO OR WHAT ARE YOU **PRAYING** FOR?

_____
_____
_____
_____
_____
_____

Scripture

WHAT QUESTION WILL YOU TAKE TO THE SCRIPTURES?

_____
_____
_____
_____

FAMILY **PROTECTION** SCRIPTURE:

_____
_____
_____
_____

Sabbath

HOW WILL YOU **KEEP** THE SABBATH THIS WEEK?

HOW WILL YOU **REMEMBER** GOD & OTHERS?

HOW CAN YOU CREATE MOMENTS OF TRADITION?

Mealtime

WHAT DAY THIS WEEK IS BEST FOR AN **INTENTIONAL** MEALTIME IN YOUR HOME?

MONDAY   TUESDAY   WEDNESDAY   THURSDAY   FRIDAY   SATURDAY   SUNDAY

HOW CAN YOU LIFT **THE ONE**?

WHAT MOMENTS OF CELEBRATION OR **CONNECTION** CAN YOU CREATE DURING THIS TIME? HOW?

Other Impressions

Week of

_____

Create • Gather • Give

Prayer

AS A . . .

_____
_____
_____
_____
_____
_____

WHO OR WHAT ARE YOU **PRAYING** FOR?

_____
_____
_____
_____
_____
_____

Scripture

WHAT QUESTION WILL YOU TAKE TO THE SCRIPTURES?

_____
_____
_____
_____

FAMILY **PROTECTION** SCRIPTURE:

_____
_____
_____

Sabbath

HOW WILL YOU **KEEP** THE SABBATH THIS WEEK?

HOW WILL YOU **REMEMBER** GOD & OTHERS?

HOW CAN YOU CREATE MOMENTS OF TRADITION?

Mealtime

WHAT DAY THIS WEEK IS BEST FOR AN **INTENTIONAL** MEALTIME IN YOUR HOME?

MONDAY   TUESDAY   WEDNESDAY   THURSDAY   FRIDAY   SATURDAY   SUNDAY

HOW CAN YOU LIFT **THE ONE**?

WHAT MOMENTS OF CELEBRATION OR **CONNECTION** CAN YOU CREATE DURING THIS TIME? HOW?

Other Impressions

Week of

_____

Create • Gather • Give

Prayer

AS A . . .

WHO OR WHAT ARE YOU **PRAYING** FOR?

Scripture

WHAT QUESTION WILL YOU TAKE TO THE SCRIPTURES?

FAMILY **PROTECTION** SCRIPTURE:

Sabbath

HOW WILL YOU **KEEP** THE SABBATH THIS WEEK?

_____

_____

_____

HOW WILL YOU **REMEMBER** GOD & OTHERS?

_____

_____

_____

HOW CAN YOU CREATE MOMENTS OF TRADITION?

_____

_____

_____

Mealtime

WHAT DAY THIS WEEK IS BEST FOR AN **INTENTIONAL** MEALTIME IN YOUR HOME?

MONDAY   TUESDAY   WEDNESDAY   THURSDAY   FRIDAY   SATURDAY   SUNDAY

HOW CAN YOU LIFT **THE ONE**?

_____

_____

WHAT MOMENTS OF CELEBRATION OR **CONNECTION** CAN YOU CREATE DURING THIS TIME? HOW?

_____

_____

Other Impressions

_____

_____

Week of

_____

Create • Gather • Give

Prayer

AS A . . .

_____
_____
_____
_____
_____
_____

WHO OR WHAT ARE YOU **PRAYING** FOR?

_____
_____
_____
_____
_____
_____

Scripture

WHAT QUESTION WILL YOU TAKE TO THE SCRIPTURES?

_____
_____
_____
_____

FAMILY **PROTECTION** SCRIPTURE:

_____
_____
_____
_____

Sabbath

HOW WILL YOU **KEEP** THE SABBATH THIS WEEK?

_____

_____

_____

HOW WILL YOU **REMEMBER** GOD & OTHERS?

_____

_____

_____

HOW CAN YOU CREATE MOMENTS OF TRADITION?

_____

_____

_____

Mealtime

WHAT DAY THIS WEEK IS BEST FOR AN **INTENTIONAL** MEALTIME IN YOUR HOME?

MONDAY   TUESDAY   WEDNESDAY   THURSDAY   FRIDAY   SATURDAY   SUNDAY

HOW CAN YOU LIFT **THE ONE**?

_____

_____

WHAT MOMENTS OF CELEBRATION OR **CONNECTION** CAN YOU CREATE DURING THIS TIME? HOW?

_____

_____

Other Impressions

_____

_____

Week of

_____

Create • Gather • Give

Prayer

AS A . . .

_____
_____
_____
_____
_____
_____

WHO OR WHAT ARE YOU **PRAYING** FOR?

_____
_____
_____
_____
_____
_____

Scripture

WHAT QUESTION WILL YOU TAKE TO THE SCRIPTURES?

_____
_____
_____
_____

FAMILY **PROTECTION** SCRIPTURE:

_____
_____
_____

Sabbath

HOW WILL YOU **KEEP** THE SABBATH THIS WEEK?

_____

_____

_____

HOW WILL YOU **REMEMBER** GOD & OTHERS?

_____

_____

_____

HOW CAN YOU CREATE MOMENTS OF TRADITION?

_____

_____

_____

Mealtime

WHAT DAY THIS WEEK IS BEST FOR AN **INTENTIONAL** MEALTIME IN YOUR HOME?

MONDAY   TUESDAY   WEDNESDAY   THURSDAY   FRIDAY   SATURDAY   SUNDAY

HOW CAN YOU LIFT **THE ONE**?

_____

_____

WHAT MOMENTS OF CELEBRATION OR **CONNECTION** CAN YOU CREATE DURING THIS TIME? HOW?

_____

_____

Other Impressions

_____

_____

Week of

_____

Create • Gather • Give

Prayer

AS A . . .

_____
_____
_____
_____
_____
_____

WHO OR WHAT ARE YOU **PRAYING** FOR?

_____
_____
_____
_____
_____
_____

Scripture

WHAT QUESTION WILL YOU TAKE TO THE SCRIPTURES?

_____
_____
_____
_____

FAMILY **PROTECTION** SCRIPTURE:

_____
_____
_____

Sabbath

HOW WILL YOU **KEEP** THE SABBATH THIS WEEK?

_____

_____

_____

HOW WILL YOU **REMEMBER** GOD & OTHERS?

_____

_____

_____

HOW CAN YOU CREATE MOMENTS OF TRADITION?

_____

_____

_____

Mealtime

WHAT DAY THIS WEEK IS BEST FOR AN **INTENTIONAL** MEALTIME IN YOUR HOME?

MONDAY   TUESDAY   WEDNESDAY   THURSDAY   FRIDAY   SATURDAY   SUNDAY

HOW CAN YOU LIFT **THE ONE**?

_____

_____

WHAT MOMENTS OF CELEBRATION OR **CONNECTION** CAN YOU CREATE DURING THIS TIME? HOW?

_____

_____

Other Impressions

_____

_____

Week of

_____

Create • Gather • Give

Prayer

AS A . . .

_____
_____
_____
_____
_____

WHO OR WHAT ARE YOU **PRAYING** FOR?

_____
_____
_____
_____
_____

Scripture

WHAT QUESTION WILL YOU TAKE TO THE SCRIPTURES?

_____
_____
_____
_____

FAMILY **PROTECTION** SCRIPTURE:

_____
_____
_____
_____

Sabbath

HOW WILL YOU **KEEP** THE SABBATH THIS WEEK?

_____

_____

_____

HOW WILL YOU **REMEMBER** GOD & OTHERS?

_____

_____

_____

HOW CAN YOU CREATE MOMENTS OF TRADITION?

_____

_____

_____

Mealtime

WHAT DAY THIS WEEK IS BEST FOR AN **INTENTIONAL** MEALTIME IN YOUR HOME?

MONDAY   TUESDAY   WEDNESDAY   THURSDAY   FRIDAY   SATURDAY   SUNDAY

HOW CAN YOU LIFT **THE ONE**?

_____

_____

WHAT MOMENTS OF CELEBRATION OR **CONNECTION** CAN YOU CREATE DURING THIS TIME? HOW?

_____

_____

Other Impressions

_____

_____

Week of

_____

Create • Gather • Give

Prayer

AS A . . .

_____
_____
_____
_____
_____
_____

WHO OR WHAT ARE YOU **PRAYING** FOR?

_____
_____
_____
_____
_____
_____

Scripture

WHAT QUESTION WILL YOU TAKE TO THE SCRIPTURES?

_____
_____
_____
_____

FAMILY **PROTECTION** SCRIPTURE:

_____
_____
_____
_____

Sabbath

HOW WILL YOU **KEEP** THE SABBATH THIS WEEK?

_____

_____

_____

HOW WILL YOU **REMEMBER** GOD & OTHERS?

_____

_____

_____

HOW CAN YOU CREATE MOMENTS OF TRADITION?

_____

_____

_____

Mealtime

WHAT DAY THIS WEEK IS BEST FOR AN **INTENTIONAL** MEALTIME IN YOUR HOME?

MONDAY   TUESDAY   WEDNESDAY   THURSDAY   FRIDAY   SATURDAY   SUNDAY

HOW CAN YOU LIFT **THE ONE**?

_____

_____

WHAT MOMENTS OF CELEBRATION OR **CONNECTION** CAN YOU CREATE DURING THIS TIME? HOW?

_____

_____

Other Impressions

_____

_____

Week of

_____

Create • Gather • Give

Prayer

AS A . . .

_____
_____
_____
_____
_____
_____

WHO OR WHAT ARE YOU **PRAYING** FOR?

_____
_____
_____
_____
_____
_____

Scripture

WHAT QUESTION WILL YOU TAKE TO THE SCRIPTURES?

_____
_____
_____
_____

FAMILY **PROTECTION** SCRIPTURE:

_____
_____
_____
_____

Sabbath

HOW WILL YOU **KEEP** THE SABBATH THIS WEEK?

_____

_____

_____

HOW WILL YOU **REMEMBER** GOD & OTHERS?

_____

_____

_____

HOW CAN YOU CREATE MOMENTS OF TRADITION?

_____

_____

_____

Mealtime

WHAT DAY THIS WEEK IS BEST FOR AN **INTENTIONAL** MEALTIME IN YOUR HOME?

MONDAY   TUESDAY   WEDNESDAY   THURSDAY   FRIDAY   SATURDAY   SUNDAY

HOW CAN YOU LIFT **THE ONE**?

_____

_____

WHAT MOMENTS OF CELEBRATION OR **CONNECTION** CAN YOU CREATE DURING THIS TIME? HOW?

_____

_____

Other Impressions

_____

_____

Week of

_____

Create • Gather • Give

Prayer

AS A . . .

WHO OR WHAT ARE YOU **PRAYING** FOR?

Scripture

WHAT QUESTION WILL YOU TAKE TO THE SCRIPTURES?

FAMILY **PROTECTION** SCRIPTURE:

Sabbath

HOW WILL YOU **KEEP** THE SABBATH THIS WEEK?

_____

_____

_____

HOW WILL YOU **REMEMBER** GOD & OTHERS?

_____

_____

HOW CAN YOU CREATE MOMENTS OF TRADITION?

_____

_____

Mealtime

WHAT DAY THIS WEEK IS BEST FOR AN **INTENTIONAL** MEALTIME IN YOUR HOME?

MONDAY   TUESDAY   WEDNESDAY   THURSDAY   FRIDAY   SATURDAY   SUNDAY

HOW CAN YOU LIFT **THE ONE**?

_____

_____

WHAT MOMENTS OF CELEBRATION OR **CONNECTION** CAN YOU CREATE DURING THIS TIME? HOW?

_____

_____

Other Impressions

_____

_____

Week of

_____

Create • Gather • Give

Prayer

AS A . . .

_____
_____
_____
_____
_____
_____

WHO OR WHAT ARE YOU **PRAYING** FOR?

_____
_____
_____
_____
_____
_____

Scripture

WHAT QUESTION WILL YOU TAKE TO THE SCRIPTURES?

_____
_____
_____
_____

FAMILY **PROTECTION** SCRIPTURE:

_____
_____
_____

Sabbath

HOW WILL YOU **KEEP** THE SABBATH THIS WEEK?

_____

_____

_____

HOW WILL YOU **REMEMBER** GOD & OTHERS?

_____

_____

_____

HOW CAN YOU CREATE MOMENTS OF TRADITION?

_____

_____

_____

Mealtime

WHAT DAY THIS WEEK IS BEST FOR AN **INTENTIONAL** MEALTIME IN YOUR HOME?

MONDAY   TUESDAY   WEDNESDAY   THURSDAY   FRIDAY   SATURDAY   SUNDAY

HOW CAN YOU LIFT **THE ONE**?

_____

_____

WHAT MOMENTS OF CELEBRATION OR **CONNECTION** CAN YOU CREATE DURING THIS TIME? HOW?

_____

_____

Other Impressions

_____

_____

Week of

_____

Create • Gather • Give

Prayer

AS A . . .

_____
_____
_____
_____
_____
_____

WHO OR WHAT ARE YOU **PRAYING** FOR?

_____
_____
_____
_____
_____
_____

Scripture

WHAT QUESTION WILL YOU TAKE TO THE SCRIPTURES?

_____
_____
_____
_____

FAMILY **PROTECTION** SCRIPTURE:

_____
_____
_____
_____

Sabbath

HOW WILL YOU **KEEP** THE SABBATH THIS WEEK?

_____

_____

_____

HOW WILL YOU **REMEMBER** GOD & OTHERS?

_____

_____

_____

HOW CAN YOU CREATE MOMENTS OF TRADITION?

_____

_____

_____

Mealtime

WHAT DAY THIS WEEK IS BEST FOR AN **INTENTIONAL** MEALTIME IN YOUR HOME?

MONDAY   TUESDAY   WEDNESDAY   THURSDAY   FRIDAY   SATURDAY   SUNDAY

HOW CAN YOU LIFT **THE ONE**?

_____

_____

WHAT MOMENTS OF CELEBRATION OR **CONNECTION** CAN YOU CREATE DURING THIS TIME? HOW?

_____

_____

Other Impressions

_____

_____

Week of

_____

Create • Gather • Give

Prayer

AS A . . .

_____
_____
_____
_____
_____
_____

WHO OR WHAT ARE YOU **PRAYING** FOR?

_____
_____
_____
_____
_____
_____

Scripture

WHAT QUESTION WILL YOU TAKE TO THE SCRIPTURES?

_____
_____
_____
_____

FAMILY **PROTECTION** SCRIPTURE:

_____
_____
_____

Sabbath

HOW WILL YOU **KEEP** THE SABBATH THIS WEEK?

_____

_____

_____

HOW WILL YOU **REMEMBER** GOD & OTHERS?

_____

_____

_____

HOW CAN YOU CREATE MOMENTS OF TRADITION?

_____

_____

_____

Mealtime

WHAT DAY THIS WEEK IS BEST FOR AN **INTENTIONAL** MEALTIME IN YOUR HOME?

MONDAY   TUESDAY   WEDNESDAY   THURSDAY   FRIDAY   SATURDAY   SUNDAY

HOW CAN YOU LIFT **THE ONE**?

_____

_____

WHAT MOMENTS OF CELEBRATION OR **CONNECTION** CAN YOU CREATE DURING THIS TIME? HOW?

_____

_____

Other Impressions

_____

_____

RITES OF PASSAGE

Gathering Event

Gathering Date

Create

WHAT IS THE PURPOSE?

_____
_____
_____
_____
_____
_____
_____

Gather

WHO IS INVITED?

_____
_____
_____
_____
_____
_____
_____

Give

HOW WILL LOVE BE EXPRESSED?

_____
_____
_____
_____
_____
_____
_____

The Experience

WHAT THEME COULD YOUR GATHERING HAVE?

_____
_____
_____

HOW WILL YOU EXTEND THE INVITATION?

☐ IN PERSON

☐ DIGITALLY

☐ BY MAIL

WHAT IS A MEANINGFUL WAY GUESTS CAN CONNECT?

_____
_____
_____

Preparing the Table

WHAT WILL YOU SERVE? ARE THERE FAMILY RECIPES THAT WOULD MAKE THIS GATHERING SPECIAL? WHAT CAN YOU PREPARE IN ADVANCE SO YOU CAN SPEND TIME CONNECTING WITH OTHERS?

Making It Memorable

WHAT DO YOU WANT THOSE GATHERING TO REMEMBER ABOUT BEING TOGETHER?

IS THERE A DECORATION, ACTIVITY, OR SPECIAL LOCATION THAT WOULD HELP CREATE THIS EXPERIENCE?

Record and Reflect

WHAT HAPPY MEMORIES WERE CREATED?

IS THERE ANYTHING YOU WOULD DO DIFFERENTLY?

Gathering Event

Gathering Date

Create

WHAT IS THE PURPOSE?

_____
_____
_____
_____
_____
_____

Gather

WHO IS INVITED?

_____
_____
_____
_____
_____
_____

Give

HOW WILL LOVE BE EXPRESSED?

_____
_____
_____
_____
_____
_____

The Experience

WHAT THEME COULD YOUR GATHERING HAVE?

_____
_____
_____

HOW WILL YOU EXTEND THE INVITATION?

☐ IN PERSON

☐ DIGITALLY

☐ BY MAIL

WHAT IS A MEANINGFUL WAY GUESTS CAN CONNECT?

_____
_____
_____

Preparing the Table

WHAT WILL YOU SERVE? ARE THERE FAMILY RECIPES THAT WOULD MAKE THIS GATHERING SPECIAL? WHAT CAN YOU PREPARE IN ADVANCE SO YOU CAN SPEND TIME CONNECTING WITH OTHERS?

_____
_____
_____

Making It Memorable

WHAT DO YOU WANT THOSE GATHERING TO REMEMBER ABOUT BEING TOGETHER?

_____
_____

IS THERE A DECORATION, ACTIVITY, OR SPECIAL LOCATION THAT WOULD HELP CREATE THIS EXPERIENCE?

_____
_____

Record and Reflect

WHAT HAPPY MEMORIES WERE CREATED? _____
_____

IS THERE ANYTHING YOU WOULD DO DIFFERENTLY? _____
_____

Gathering Event

Gathering Date

Create

WHAT IS THE PURPOSE?

_____

_____

_____

_____

_____

_____

Gather

WHO IS INVITED?

_____

_____

_____

_____

_____

_____

Give

HOW WILL LOVE BE EXPRESSED?

_____

_____

_____

_____

_____

_____

The Experience

WHAT THEME COULD YOUR GATHERING HAVE?

_____

_____

_____

HOW WILL YOU EXTEND THE INVITATION?

☐ IN PERSON

☐ DIGITALLY

☐ BY MAIL

WHAT IS A MEANINGFUL WAY GUESTS CAN CONNECT?

_____

_____

_____

Preparing the Table

WHAT WILL YOU SERVE? ARE THERE FAMILY RECIPES THAT WOULD MAKE THIS GATHERING SPECIAL? WHAT CAN YOU PREPARE IN ADVANCE SO YOU CAN SPEND TIME CONNECTING WITH OTHERS?

_____

_____

_____

Making It Memorable

WHAT DO YOU WANT THOSE GATHERING TO REMEMBER ABOUT BEING TOGETHER?

_____

_____

IS THERE A DECORATION, ACTIVITY, OR SPECIAL LOCATION THAT WOULD HELP CREATE THIS EXPERIENCE?

_____

_____

Record and Reflect

WHAT HAPPY MEMORIES WERE CREATED? _____

_____

IS THERE ANYTHING YOU WOULD DO DIFFERENTLY? _____

_____

THE CELEBRATION OF SEASONS

Gathering Event _____   Gathering Date _____

Create

WHAT IS THE PURPOSE?

_____
_____
_____
_____
_____
_____

Gather

WHO IS INVITED?

_____
_____
_____
_____
_____
_____

Give

HOW WILL LOVE BE EXPRESSED?

_____
_____
_____
_____
_____
_____

The Experience

WHAT THEME COULD YOUR GATHERING HAVE?

_____
_____
_____

HOW WILL YOU EXTEND THE INVITATION?

☐ IN PERSON
☐ DIGITALLY
☐ BY MAIL

WHAT IS A MEANINGFUL WAY GUESTS CAN CONNECT?

_____
_____
_____

Preparing the Table

WHAT WILL YOU SERVE? ARE THERE FAMILY RECIPES THAT WOULD MAKE THIS GATHERING SPECIAL? WHAT CAN YOU PREPARE IN ADVANCE SO YOU CAN SPEND TIME CONNECTING WITH OTHERS?

_____

_____

_____

Making It Memorable

WHAT DO YOU WANT THOSE GATHERING TO REMEMBER ABOUT BEING TOGETHER?

_____

_____

IS THERE A DECORATION, ACTIVITY, OR SPECIAL LOCATION THAT WOULD HELP CREATE THIS EXPERIENCE?

_____

_____

Record and Reflect

WHAT HAPPY MEMORIES WERE CREATED? _____

_____

IS THERE ANYTHING YOU WOULD DO DIFFERENTLY? _____

_____

Gathering Event

Gathering Date

Create

WHAT IS THE PURPOSE?

_____

_____

_____

_____

_____

_____

Gather

WHO IS INVITED?

_____

_____

_____

_____

_____

_____

Give

HOW WILL LOVE BE EXPRESSED?

_____

_____

_____

_____

_____

_____

The Experience

WHAT THEME COULD YOUR GATHERING HAVE?

_____

_____

_____

HOW WILL YOU EXTEND THE INVITATION?

☐ IN PERSON

☐ DIGITALLY

☐ BY MAIL

WHAT IS A MEANINGFUL WAY GUESTS CAN CONNECT?

_____

_____

Preparing the Table

WHAT WILL YOU SERVE? ARE THERE FAMILY RECIPES THAT WOULD MAKE THIS GATHERING SPECIAL? WHAT CAN YOU PREPARE IN ADVANCE SO YOU CAN SPEND TIME CONNECTING WITH OTHERS?

_____

_____

_____

Making It Memorable

WHAT DO YOU WANT THOSE GATHERING TO REMEMBER ABOUT BEING TOGETHER?

_____

_____

IS THERE A DECORATION, ACTIVITY, OR SPECIAL LOCATION THAT WOULD HELP CREATE THIS EXPERIENCE?

_____

_____

Record and Reflect

WHAT HAPPY MEMORIES WERE CREATED? _____

_____

IS THERE ANYTHING YOU WOULD DO DIFFERENTLY? _____

_____

Gathering Event _____ Gathering Date _____

Create

WHAT IS THE PURPOSE?

_____
_____
_____
_____
_____
_____

Gather

WHO IS INVITED?

_____
_____
_____
_____
_____
_____

Give

HOW WILL LOVE BE EXPRESSED?

_____
_____
_____
_____
_____
_____

The Experience

WHAT THEME COULD YOUR GATHERING HAVE?

_____
_____
_____

HOW WILL YOU EXTEND THE INVITATION?

☐ IN PERSON
☐ DIGITALLY
☐ BY MAIL

WHAT IS A MEANINGFUL WAY GUESTS CAN CONNECT?

_____
_____
_____

Preparing the Table

WHAT WILL YOU SERVE? ARE THERE FAMILY RECIPES THAT WOULD MAKE THIS GATHERING SPECIAL? WHAT CAN YOU PREPARE IN ADVANCE SO YOU CAN SPEND TIME CONNECTING WITH OTHERS?

_____
_____
_____
_____

Making It Memorable

WHAT DO YOU WANT THOSE GATHERING TO REMEMBER ABOUT BEING TOGETHER?

_____
_____

IS THERE A DECORATION, ACTIVITY, OR SPECIAL LOCATION THAT WOULD HELP CREATE THIS EXPERIENCE?

_____
_____

Record and Reflect

WHAT HAPPY MEMORIES WERE CREATED? _____
_____

IS THERE ANYTHING YOU WOULD DO DIFFERENTLY? _____
_____

Gathering Event

Gathering Date

Create

WHAT IS THE PURPOSE?

_____

_____

_____

_____

_____

_____

Gather

WHO IS INVITED?

_____

_____

_____

_____

_____

_____

Give

HOW WILL LOVE BE EXPRESSED?

_____

_____

_____

_____

_____

_____

The Experience

WHAT THEME COULD YOUR GATHERING HAVE?

_____

_____

_____

HOW WILL YOU EXTEND THE INVITATION?

☐ IN PERSON

☐ DIGITALLY

☐ BY MAIL

WHAT IS A MEANINGFUL WAY GUESTS CAN CONNECT?

_____

_____

_____

Preparing the Table

WHAT WILL YOU SERVE? ARE THERE FAMILY RECIPES THAT WOULD MAKE THIS GATHERING SPECIAL? WHAT CAN YOU PREPARE IN ADVANCE SO YOU CAN SPEND TIME CONNECTING WITH OTHERS?

_____

_____

_____

_____

Making It Memorable

WHAT DO YOU WANT THOSE GATHERING TO REMEMBER ABOUT BEING TOGETHER?

_____

_____

IS THERE A DECORATION, ACTIVITY, OR SPECIAL LOCATION THAT WOULD HELP CREATE THIS EXPERIENCE?

_____

_____

Record and Reflect

WHAT HAPPY MEMORIES WERE CREATED? _____

_____

IS THERE ANYTHING YOU WOULD DO DIFFERENTLY? _____

_____

Gathering Event   Gathering Date

Create

WHAT IS THE PURPOSE?

_____

_____

_____

_____

_____

_____

Gather

WHO IS INVITED?

_____

_____

_____

_____

_____

_____

Give

HOW WILL LOVE BE EXPRESSED?

_____

_____

_____

_____

_____

_____

The Experience

WHAT THEME COULD YOUR GATHERING HAVE?

_____

_____

_____

HOW WILL YOU EXTEND THE INVITATION?

☐ IN PERSON

☐ DIGITALLY

☐ BY MAIL

WHAT IS A MEANINGFUL WAY GUESTS CAN CONNECT?

_____

_____

_____

Preparing the Table

WHAT WILL YOU SERVE? ARE THERE FAMILY RECIPES THAT WOULD MAKE THIS GATHERING SPECIAL? WHAT CAN YOU PREPARE IN ADVANCE SO YOU CAN SPEND TIME CONNECTING WITH OTHERS?

_____

_____

_____

Making It Memorable

WHAT DO YOU WANT THOSE GATHERING TO REMEMBER ABOUT BEING TOGETHER?

_____

_____

IS THERE A DECORATION, ACTIVITY, OR SPECIAL LOCATION THAT WOULD HELP CREATE THIS EXPERIENCE?

_____

_____

Record and Reflect

WHAT HAPPY MEMORIES WERE CREATED? _____

_____

IS THERE ANYTHING YOU WOULD DO DIFFERENTLY? _____

_____

Gathering Event   Gathering Date

Create

WHAT IS THE PURPOSE?

_____

_____

_____

_____

_____

_____

Gather

WHO IS INVITED?

_____

_____

_____

_____

_____

_____

Give

HOW WILL LOVE BE EXPRESSED?

_____

_____

_____

_____

_____

_____

The Experience

WHAT THEME COULD YOUR GATHERING HAVE?

_____

_____

_____

HOW WILL YOU EXTEND THE INVITATION?

☐ IN PERSON

☐ DIGITALLY

☐ BY MAIL

WHAT IS A MEANINGFUL WAY GUESTS CAN CONNECT?

_____

_____

_____

Preparing the Table

WHAT WILL YOU SERVE? ARE THERE FAMILY RECIPES THAT WOULD MAKE THIS GATHERING SPECIAL? WHAT CAN YOU PREPARE IN ADVANCE SO YOU CAN SPEND TIME CONNECTING WITH OTHERS?

_____

_____

_____

Making It Memorable

WHAT DO YOU WANT THOSE GATHERING TO REMEMBER ABOUT BEING TOGETHER?

_____

_____

IS THERE A DECORATION, ACTIVITY, OR SPECIAL LOCATION THAT WOULD HELP CREATE THIS EXPERIENCE?

_____

_____

Record and Reflect

WHAT HAPPY MEMORIES WERE CREATED? _____

_____

IS THERE ANYTHING YOU WOULD DO DIFFERENTLY? _____

_____

Gathering Event _____   Gathering Date _____

Create

WHAT IS THE PURPOSE?

_____
_____
_____
_____
_____
_____

Gather

WHO IS INVITED?

_____
_____
_____
_____
_____
_____

Give

HOW WILL LOVE BE EXPRESSED?

_____
_____
_____
_____
_____
_____

The Experience

WHAT THEME COULD YOUR GATHERING HAVE?

_____
_____
_____

HOW WILL YOU EXTEND THE INVITATION?

☐ IN PERSON
☐ DIGITALLY
☐ BY MAIL

WHAT IS A MEANINGFUL WAY GUESTS CAN CONNECT?

_____
_____
_____

Preparing the Table

WHAT WILL YOU SERVE? ARE THERE FAMILY RECIPES THAT WOULD MAKE THIS GATHERING SPECIAL? WHAT CAN YOU PREPARE IN ADVANCE SO YOU CAN SPEND TIME CONNECTING WITH OTHERS?

_____

_____

_____

Making It Memorable

WHAT DO YOU WANT THOSE GATHERING TO REMEMBER ABOUT BEING TOGETHER?

_____

_____

IS THERE A DECORATION, ACTIVITY, OR SPECIAL LOCATION THAT WOULD HELP CREATE THIS EXPERIENCE?

_____

_____

Record and Reflect

WHAT HAPPY MEMORIES WERE CREATED? _____

_____

IS THERE ANYTHING YOU WOULD DO DIFFERENTLY? _____

_____

Gathering Event   Gathering Date

_____   _____

Create

WHAT IS THE PURPOSE?

_____
_____
_____
_____
_____
_____

Gather

WHO IS INVITED?

_____
_____
_____
_____
_____
_____

Give

HOW WILL LOVE BE EXPRESSED?

_____
_____
_____
_____
_____
_____

The Experience

WHAT THEME COULD YOUR GATHERING HAVE?

_____
_____
_____

HOW WILL YOU EXTEND THE INVITATION?

☐ IN PERSON

☐ DIGITALLY

☐ BY MAIL

WHAT IS A MEANINGFUL WAY GUESTS CAN CONNECT?

_____
_____
_____

Preparing the Table

WHAT WILL YOU SERVE? ARE THERE FAMILY RECIPES THAT WOULD MAKE THIS GATHERING SPECIAL? WHAT CAN YOU PREPARE IN ADVANCE SO YOU CAN SPEND TIME CONNECTING WITH OTHERS?

_____

_____

_____

_____

Making It Memorable

WHAT DO YOU WANT THOSE GATHERING TO REMEMBER ABOUT BEING TOGETHER?

_____

_____

IS THERE A DECORATION, ACTIVITY, OR SPECIAL LOCATION THAT WOULD HELP CREATE THIS EXPERIENCE?

_____

_____

Record and Reflect

WHAT HAPPY MEMORIES WERE CREATED? _____

_____

IS THERE ANYTHING YOU WOULD DO DIFFERENTLY? _____

_____

Gathering Event

Gathering Date

Create

WHAT IS THE PURPOSE?

_____
_____
_____
_____
_____
_____

Gather

WHO IS INVITED?

_____
_____
_____
_____
_____
_____

Give

HOW WILL LOVE BE EXPRESSED?

_____
_____
_____
_____
_____
_____

The Experience

WHAT THEME COULD YOUR GATHERING HAVE?

_____
_____
_____

HOW WILL YOU EXTEND THE INVITATION?

☐ IN PERSON

☐ DIGITALLY

☐ BY MAIL

WHAT IS A MEANINGFUL WAY GUESTS CAN CONNECT?

_____
_____
_____

Preparing the Table

WHAT WILL YOU SERVE? ARE THERE FAMILY RECIPES THAT WOULD MAKE THIS GATHERING SPECIAL? WHAT CAN YOU PREPARE IN ADVANCE SO YOU CAN SPEND TIME CONNECTING WITH OTHERS?

_____

_____

_____

Making It Memorable

WHAT DO YOU WANT THOSE GATHERING TO REMEMBER ABOUT BEING TOGETHER?

_____

_____

IS THERE A DECORATION, ACTIVITY, OR SPECIAL LOCATION THAT WOULD HELP CREATE THIS EXPERIENCE?

_____

_____

Record and Reflect

WHAT HAPPY MEMORIES WERE CREATED? _____

_____

IS THERE ANYTHING YOU WOULD DO DIFFERENTLY? _____

_____

Gathering Event

Gathering Date

Create

WHAT IS THE PURPOSE?

_____
_____
_____
_____
_____
_____

Gather

WHO IS INVITED?

_____
_____
_____
_____
_____
_____

Give

HOW WILL LOVE BE EXPRESSED?

_____
_____
_____
_____
_____
_____

The Experience

WHAT THEME COULD YOUR GATHERING HAVE?

_____
_____
_____

HOW WILL YOU EXTEND THE INVITATION?

☐ IN PERSON

☐ DIGITALLY

☐ BY MAIL

WHAT IS A MEANINGFUL WAY GUESTS CAN CONNECT?

_____
_____
_____

Preparing the Table

WHAT WILL YOU SERVE? ARE THERE FAMILY RECIPES THAT WOULD MAKE THIS GATHERING SPECIAL? WHAT CAN YOU PREPARE IN ADVANCE SO YOU CAN SPEND TIME CONNECTING WITH OTHERS?

_____

_____

_____

_____

Making It Memorable

WHAT DO YOU WANT THOSE GATHERING TO REMEMBER ABOUT BEING TOGETHER?

_____

_____

IS THERE A DECORATION, ACTIVITY, OR SPECIAL LOCATION THAT WOULD HELP CREATE THIS EXPERIENCE?

_____

_____

Record and Reflect

WHAT HAPPY MEMORIES WERE CREATED? _____

_____

IS THERE ANYTHING YOU WOULD DO DIFFERENTLY? _____

_____

Gathering Event

Gathering Date

Create

WHAT IS THE PURPOSE?

_____
_____
_____
_____
_____
_____

Gather

WHO IS INVITED?

_____
_____
_____
_____
_____
_____

Give

HOW WILL LOVE BE EXPRESSED?

_____
_____
_____
_____
_____
_____

The Experience

WHAT THEME COULD YOUR GATHERING HAVE?

_____
_____
_____

HOW WILL YOU EXTEND THE INVITATION?

☐ IN PERSON

☐ DIGITALLY

☐ BY MAIL

WHAT IS A MEANINGFUL WAY GUESTS CAN CONNECT?

_____
_____
_____

Preparing the Table

WHAT WILL YOU SERVE? ARE THERE FAMILY RECIPES THAT WOULD MAKE THIS GATHERING SPECIAL? WHAT CAN YOU PREPARE IN ADVANCE SO YOU CAN SPEND TIME CONNECTING WITH OTHERS?

_____
_____
_____
_____

Making It Memorable

WHAT DO YOU WANT THOSE GATHERING TO REMEMBER ABOUT BEING TOGETHER?

_____
_____

IS THERE A DECORATION, ACTIVITY, OR SPECIAL LOCATION THAT WOULD HELP CREATE THIS EXPERIENCE?

_____
_____

Record and Reflect

WHAT HAPPY MEMORIES WERE CREATED? _____
_____

IS THERE ANYTHING YOU WOULD DO DIFFERENTLY? _____
_____

Gathering Event _____   Gathering Date _____

Create

WHAT IS THE PURPOSE?

_____
_____
_____
_____
_____

Gather

WHO IS INVITED?

_____
_____
_____
_____
_____

Give

HOW WILL LOVE BE EXPRESSED?

_____
_____
_____
_____
_____

The Experience

WHAT THEME COULD YOUR GATHERING HAVE?

_____
_____

HOW WILL YOU EXTEND THE INVITATION?

☐ IN PERSON
☐ DIGITALLY
☐ BY MAIL

WHAT IS A MEANINGFUL WAY GUESTS CAN CONNECT?

_____
_____

Preparing the Table

WHAT WILL YOU SERVE? ARE THERE FAMILY RECIPES THAT WOULD MAKE THIS GATHERING SPECIAL? WHAT CAN YOU PREPARE IN ADVANCE SO YOU CAN SPEND TIME CONNECTING WITH OTHERS?

_____

_____

_____

_____

Making It Memorable

WHAT DO YOU WANT THOSE GATHERING TO REMEMBER ABOUT BEING TOGETHER?

_____

_____

IS THERE A DECORATION, ACTIVITY, OR SPECIAL LOCATION THAT WOULD HELP CREATE THIS EXPERIENCE?

_____

_____

Record and Reflect

WHAT HAPPY MEMORIES WERE CREATED? _____

_____

IS THERE ANYTHING YOU WOULD DO DIFFERENTLY? _____

_____

GENERAL CONFERENCE

General Conference

DATES

Saturday   Sunday

HOW WILL YOU MAKE SPACE FOR LEARNING?

WHAT ARE YOUR MEAL TRADITIONS OR SNACK IDEAS?

WHAT ACTIVITIES COULD YOU DO BETWEEN SESSIONS?

Simple Ways to Create a Weekend Sanctuary of Holiness

Family Question or Need for This Conference

Standout Quote from This Conference

General Conference

DATES _____

Saturday   Sunday

HOW WILL YOU MAKE SPACE FOR LEARNING?

WHAT ARE YOUR MEAL TRADITIONS OR SNACK IDEAS?

WHAT ACTIVITIES COULD YOU DO BETWEEN SESSIONS?

Simple Ways to Create a Weekend Sanctuary of Holiness

Family Question or Need for This Conference

Standout Quote from This Conference

References

p. 13, **Assaults of the adversary are increasing**: Russell M. Nelson, "Becoming Exemplary Latter-day Saints," *Ensign*, November 2018.

p. 22, **The prophet has asked each of us to do the same**: see Nelson, "Becoming Exemplary Latter-day Saints."

p. 31, **I remember my mother's prayers**: Abraham Lincoln, *The Lincoln Year Book: Axioms and Aphorisms from the Great Emancipator*, comp. Wallace Rice (Chicago: A.C. McClurg & Co., 1907), May 20.

p. 35, **He who reads it oftenest will like it best**: Joseph Smith, *Teachings of Presidents of the Church: Joseph Smith* (Salt Lake City: The Church of Jesus Christ of Latter-day Saints, 2011), 56.

p. 39, **A world without a Sabbath**: Henry Ward Beecher, as quoted in Joseph S. Exell, ed., *Biblical Illustrator Commentary*, vol. 1 (n.p.: Delmarva Publications, 2015).

pp. 39–40, **How can you ensure that your behavior on the Sabbath**: Russell M. Nelson, "The Sabbath Is a Delight," *Ensign*, May 2015.

p. 41, **Changes in your family will be dramatic and sustaining**: Nelson, "Becoming Exemplary Latter-day Saints."

p. 43, **Where there is love there is life**: Original source unknown. Attributed to Mahatma Gandhi.

p. 43, **Perhaps nothing in the life of a household**: *Cassell's Book of the Household: A Work of Reference on Domestic Economy* (Cassell: London, 1889).

p. 55, **George Durrant once wrote a book**: see George D. Durrant, *My Best Day So Far: A How-To Book on Happiness* (Salt Lake City: Bookcraft, 1990).

p. 59, **A good life is a collection of happy memories**: Denis Waitley, Facebook, March 26, 2014, https://www.facebook.com/OfficialDenisWaitley/posts/a-good-life-is-a-collection-of-happy-memories-denis-waitley/702905939752736/.

p. 63, **Home should be an anchor**: Marvin J. Ashton, "A Yearning for Home," *Ensign*, November 1992.

p. 69, **Create of your homes sanctuaries of holiness and strength**: Joseph B. Wirthlin, "The Abundant Life," *Ensign*, May 2006.

p. 74, **'Twas Easter-Sunday**: Henry Wadsworth Longfellow, *The Spanish Student*, in *The Complete Poetical Works of Henry W. Longfellow* (Edinburgh and London: Gall & Inglis, 1870), 36.

p. 79, **I sustain myself with the love of family**: Maya Angelou, Facebook, November 3, 2019, https://www.facebook.com/MayaAngelou/posts/10158619771634796.

p. 83, **We were together**: Walt Whitman, *Leaves of Grass* (Boston: Thayer and Eldridge, 1860), 311.

p. 89, **Celebrate . . . each day together**: Russell M. Nelson, "Nurturing Marriage," *Ensign*, May 2006.

p. 93, **The happy life is not ushered in at any age**: Thomas S. Monson, "Attitudes of Accomplishment" (devotional, Brigham Young University, Provo, Utah, May 19, 1970).

p. 93, **Make no small plans**: Spencer W. Kimball, as quoted in Vaughn J. Featherstone, "The Last Drop in the Chalice" (devotional, Brigham Young University, Provo, Utah, September 24, 1985).

p. 99, **This is the power of gathering**: Alice Waters, *40 Years of Chez Panisse: The Power of Gathering* (New York: Clarkson Potter, 2011).

p. 103, **Every day in your life is a special occasion**: Quoted in Thomas S. Monson, "In Search of Treasure," *Ensign*, May 2003.

p. 108, **Gratitude is said to be the memory of the heart**: Joseph F. Smith, *Gospel Doctrine: The Sermons and Writings of Joseph F. Smith*, 5th ed. (Salt Lake City: Deseret Book, 1939), 262.

p. 115, **Christmastime is cherished family time**: Russell M. Nelson, "Jesus the Christ—Our Prince of Peace" (Christmas devotional, Conference Center, Salt Lake City, December 8, 2013).